Farmhouse Classics

Pickles, Chutneys & Preserves

Alison Lingard

FARMHOUSE CLASSICS – PICKLES, CHUTNEYS & PRESERVES
Copyright © 2014 by Alison Lingard

All rights reserved. No part of this book may be reproduced or transmitted in any form or by any means without written permission from the author.

ISBN-13: 978-1497530522
ISBN-10: 1497530520

Contents

Introduction **4**

Farmhouse Pickles **5**

Farmhouse Chutneys and Relishes **62**

Farmhouse Preserves **104**

Conversion Chart **138**

Index **140**

Introduction

With more than 125 farm favourite pickle, chutney and preserve recipes you will quickly come to realise just how delicious country living is.

The classic recipes in this collection include preserved lemons, red pickled ginger, corn relish, cherry chutney, mango chutney, farmhouse dill pickles, green tomato chutney, watermelon mint jam, strawberry vanilla preserve and spicy jalapeno pickles. With such a vast array of recipes you can expect some wild and crazy recipes too just like Grandad use to make for Sunday lunch back on the farm.

Up until now these recipes have been closely guarded secrets usually handed down from generation to generation, now however they are all laid out for you in quick and easy steps.

So whether you are looking for that perfect relish or that classic dill pickle, this book is sure to spice up your pantry with those old time favourites that have been impressing for years.

Farmhouse Pickles

Pickles are a combination of sweet, sour, salty and spicy vegetables or fruit that have been preserved in vinegar or brine.

Stored for months sometimes years pickles are a condiment that are always readily available to spice up that bland household staple.

With one of the all time favourites being the various versions of the humble pickled onion.

English Style Pickled Onions

½ cup sea salt
9 cups water
1½ kg unpeeled small onions
4 tablespoons brown sugar
4 cups malt or apple cider vinegar
1 teaspoon black peppercorns
1 teaspoon mixed or green peppercorns
½ teaspoon whole allspice
4 bay leaves, crumbled
12 whole cloves
3 small chopped and deseeded chillies

1. In a mixing bowl, dissolve ¼ cup sea salt in 4 ½ cups water. Add the onions and weigh them down gently with a plate that fits inside the bowl. They must be kept submerged.
2. Let stand for 8 to 12 hours.
3. Drain and peel the onions and return them to the bowl.
4. Make a new brine with another batch of salt and water, pour it over the onions, and weigh them down gently again.
5. Stand for 2 days.
6. In a non-reactive saucepan, bring the sugar and vinegar to a boil. Cool.
7. Drain and rinse the onions twice.
8. Mix all picking spices together and ½ fill preserving jars with onions.
9. Divide ½ the spices on top of onions.
10. Fill jars to top with remaining onions and place remaining spices on top.
11. Fill each jar of onions with the cooled, sweetened vinegar, ensuring that onions are completely covered.
12. Place the cap on the jar.
13. Refrigerate the jars for at least 1 month before eating the onions.

{preparation + cook time 45 minutes over several days makes 4 jars}

Dads Spicy Pickled Onions

1.3kg of small pickling onions
50g of sea salt
4 habanero chillies (can also use red chillies)
400 g sugar
2 tablespoons of cloves
1 tablespoon of mustard seeds
1.2 litres of white wine vinegar

1. Trim onions, then blanch under boiling water with the skins on for 20 seconds.
2. Cover with cold water and peel them while keeping them submerged under water (this prevents the onions from oxidising and toughening up).
3. Place onions in clean bowl, sprinkling well with salt. Cover and leave overnight.
4. The next day, rinse and dry the onions.
5. Put in sterilised jars with 2 halves of chilli in each jar along with spices and cloves.
6. Boil the sugar and vinegar for 1 minute and then pour over the onions.
7. Seal the jars and let rest for 3 or 4 weeks

{**preparation + cook time** 30 minutes **makes** 4 jars}

Curried Pickled Eggs

1 cup apple cider vinegar
3/4 cup water
1/4 onion, sliced
3/4 cup of white granulated sugar
3 cardamom pods
1 teaspoon of mustard seeds (yellow or brown)
1 tablespoon of yellow curry powder
6 hardboiled eggs - peeled

1. Boil the eggs until hard cooked. To boil the eggs, cover with 2 inches of cold water in a saucepan, bring to a boil, cover, remove from heat, and let sit for 12 minutes, then rinse with cold water.
2. Peel the eggs and place in the bottom of a clean glass jar.
3. In a medium saucepan, add the vinegar, water, the onion sugar, and spices.
4. Bring to a boil and cook, uncovered, until the sugar has dissolved and the onions are translucent, usually takes about 5 minutes.
5. Remove the saucepan from the heat and let cool for a few minutes.
6. Pour the vinegar onion mixture over the eggs in the jar, covering the eggs completely. Secure close the jar's cover. Refrigerate up to 3 days before eating

The pickled eggs will last for about 1 month. The longer the eggs sit in the pickling juice, the stronger the flavours will be throughout the eggs.

{**preparation + cook time** 40 minutes **makes** 6 eggs}

Farmhouse Dill Pickles

3 cucumbers (or 8 mini cucumbers)
2 cloves of garlic
2 sprigs of fresh dill
½ teaspoon coriander seeds
¼ teaspoon mustard seeds
¼ teaspoon whole peppercorns
1 pinch of red pepper flakes
2 cups of water
1 tablespoon of sea salt

1. Cut your cucumbers into your desired size. Sliced cucumbers will ferment faster than whole cucumbers. You can keep them whole if using mini cucumbers
2. Tightly pack the cucumbers into your jar
3. Add the garlic, fresh dill and all the spices on top.
4. Mix the water and sea salt together until the salt is dissolved.
5. Pour your water mix over the pickles. Leave about an inch of space between the water and the top of the jar. All the cucumbers must be submerged in the water. Weigh them down with something if you are having trouble keeping them totally submerged. My Grandma use to use onions cut in half to weigh them down as it also adds more flavour.
6. Put the lid on your jar and leave it sit at room temperature for 3 days.
7. On day 3 move the pickle jar to your fridge to stop the fermenting process
8. After a while you may see a white film on top of the pickle juice, just skim it off. It is just yeast but it will alter the taste of the pickles if you don't skim it off.
9. Your pickles will keep for 6 months in the fridge.

{**preparation + cook time** 15 minutes **makes** 1 jar}

Auntie's Pickled Artichokes

40 baby artichokes
1 cup lemon juice
2 cups white vinegar
1 cup olive oil
5 sliced garlic cloves
4 dried chilies
About a dozen juniper berries (optional)
2 bay leaves
3 teaspoons salt
4 lemons, sliced in half
2 Mason Jars

1. Put all ingredients except for the artichokes in a large pot and bring it to a rolling boil. Cover and turn off the heat.
2. Fill a stockpot with enough water to cover the amount of jars you will need to can these artichokes. You will need something on the bottom of the pot to keep the glass jars off the bottom (do not put the jars in yet). Aunty use to use spare jar rims. Put it on medium heat.
3. Get a large bowl and fill it with cold water. Squeeze 2 lemons into the water and drop the lemons into the bowl.
4. Pick off the tough outer leaves of the artichokes, leaving only the leaves that are tightly attached and yellow at the centre. Using a sharp knife, trim the outer layer off the artichoke bottom, leaving as much as you can then rub the artichoke all over with cut lemon and drop it into the bowl with the lemons. This prevents them from oxidizing and turning brown. Repeat until you are done.
5. Turn the heat back onto the pot with the seasoned vinegar and oil. Put the artichokes in that pot, stir around and bring to a boil. Allow them to boil for 3 minutes then remove from heat.
6. With a slotted spoon, fill the Mason jars 3/4 full with the artichokes. Ladle the vinegar-oil mixture over the artichokes evenly. If you run out of brine, you can add a little vinegar and oil to top off. Place the lids on the jars.
7. Carefully submerge the two jars in the now-boiling water of the stockpot. Let this boil for 15-20 minutes then remove the stockpot from the heat. Once safe enough, remove the jars from the stockpot and let cool on a cutting board until the artichokes return to room temperature. They will keep a year. Refrigerate after opening.

{preparation + cook time 1 hour 15 minutes **makes** 2 jars}

Pickled Jalapenos

100g (4 oz.) sliced green jalapeno chilies
1 cup Chinese rice vinegar
1 teaspoon salt
1/2 teaspoon sugar
1 cup water (boiled)

1. Place the sliced chilies in to a bowl (discard the seeds if you don't like them too hot).
2. Pour 1 cup of boiling water over the chilies. Drain the chilies from the boiling water after 10 seconds.
3. In the same bowl, add in the rice vinegar, salt and sugar. Stir to blend well.
4. Transfer the chilies and the liquid brine in to a glass jar and seal it.
5. Once cooled to room temperature place the jar of chilies in the fridge overnight

Keeps for up to 6 weeks in the refrigerator

{**preparation + cook time** 10 minutes **makes** 1 jar}

Red Pickled Cabbage

1 red cabbage
1/4 cup apple cider vinegar
2 tablespoons honey
1/2 cup olive oil
salt & pepper

1. Grate or shred the red cabbage into very thin slivers.
2. Place the red cabbage in to a porcelain bowl.
3. Add 1/2 cup of olive oil.
4. Add 1/4 cup of Apple cider vinegar
5. Add 3 tablespoon of raw honey.
6. Gently mix everything together and season with salt & pepper to taste.
7. Pack tightly in to glass jars and store refrigerated.

The ratio can be adjusted to your taste. If you like it tarter, add more vinegar or vice versa.

{**preparation time** 10 minutes **makes** 3 jars}

Farmhouse Preserved Lemons

8 lemons
1 ½ cups rock salt
1 teaspoon coriander leaves
4 bay leaves (preferably fresh but dry is fine)
1 teaspoon caraway seeds
1 cup lemon juice
Cinnamon sticks

1. Cut the lemons in to quarters without cutting all the way through
2. Squeeze the lemons over a bowl to extract some of the juice
3. Place the lemons in the bowl along with the salt, bay leaves and seeds, mix well
4. Pack the lemon mixture in to sterilized jars making sure you pour enough of the juice in to the jar to cover all lemons
5. Place a cinnamon stick in each jar
6. Seal the jars ensuring all lemons are submerged (weigh them down with something if needed)
7. Store lemons in a cool dark place for at least 3 weeks before consuming and refrigerate after opening

{preparation time 15 minutes makes 16 slices}

Red Pickled Ginger

250g (1/2lb) gingerroot
1 tablespoon salt
1 ¼ cups rice wine vinegar
3 tablespoons water
¼ cup sugar
1 -2 drop red food coloring

1. Wash and peel the ginger and cut it in to very thin slices. As thin as you possibly can.
2. Rub the sliced ginger with the salt until it dissolves.
3. Place the ginger in a bowl and refrigerate for 3 hours then take it out of the fridge and squeeze out as much liquid as possible.
4. Put ginger in a clean sterilized jar.
5. Place the vinegar, water, red food coloring and sugar in a small sauce pan and bring to a gentle simmer and stir gently until the sugar is completely dissolved.
6. Pour the mixture over the ginger and allow it to cool slightly before putting the lid on.
7. Place the ginger in the fridge for at least 3 days before consuming.

{**preparation time** 10 minutes **makes** 1 jar}

Grans Sweet Mustard Pickles

3 ½ L water
1 cup salt
1 large head cauliflower, chopped into bite size pieces
3kg diced onions
2 diced cucumbers
1 ½ L cider vinegar
1 cup flour
4 cups white sugar
2 tablespoons mustard powder
1 tablespoon curry powder
1 tablespoon ground turmeric

1. Combine the water and salt in a large pot. Stir until the salt is dissolved.
2. Add the cauliflower, onion, and cucumber to the pot, cover and allow to sit overnight.
3. Remove cover and bring the mixture to the boil over medium-high heat; simmer until the vegetables are tender then drain the vegetables to remove all liquid.
4. Add the vinegar, flour, sugar, mustard powder, curry powder, and turmeric to the vegetables and bring to a rolling boil; reduce the heat to low and simmer until the mixture thickens, stirring occasionally.
5. Allow to cool slightly then ladle the mixture into sterilized jars and screw on the lids. Once cooled you can serve immediately.

{**preparation time** 35 minutes **makes** 6 jars}

Bread and Butter Pickles

4 cups pickling cucumbers sliced ¼ inch thick
1 sweet onion (thinly sliced)
¼ cup salt
70g sugar
½ cup white vinegar
¼ teaspoon ground turmeric
1 tablespoon mustard seeds
1 tablespoon coriander seeds
¼ teaspoon celery seed

1. In a medium bowl combine the sliced cucumbers, onion and salt, mix gently.
2. Cover the cucumbers with ice and let stand at room temperature for two hours.
3. In a medium pot, bring the sugar, vinegar and spices to a boil.
4. Drain the cucumbers and onions then add them to the vinegar mixture and bring almost back to a boil.
5. Remove from heat and allow the mixture to cool slightly before transferring to jar and sealing the jar.
6. The pickles will be ready to eat after 4 hours and will keep refrigerated for about 6 weeks

{**preparation time** 30 minutes **makes** 1 jar}

Pickled Garlic

250g garlic (peeled)
1 red bell pepper (chopped)
2 cups apple cider vinegar
2/3 cup white sugar
½ teaspoon dry mustard (ground)
½ teaspoon celery seed

1. Place garlic cloves in a medium bowl, first cutting the large cloves in half. Mix in the red bell pepper.
2. Place the apple cider vinegar and sugar in a medium saucepan on medium high heat.
3. Wrap ground dry mustard and celery seed in a spice bag, and place in the liquid mixture.
4. Bring to a boil. Boil 5 minutes. Stir in garlic and pepper. Continue boiling 5 minutes.
5. Remove from heat and discard spice bag.
6. Place garlic and peppers in sterile jars to within 1 inch of the top. Fill with remaining liquid to within ¼ inch from the top of the jar. Seal and store in the refrigerator approximately three weeks before serving.

{**preparation time** 25 minutes **makes** 1 jar}

Pickled Carrot Sticks

6 carrots (cut into sticks)
1 ¼ cups water
1 cup cider vinegar
¼ cup sugar
2 crushed garlic cloves
1 ½ tablespoons dried dill
1 ½ tablespoons salt

1. Place carrots in a heatproof bowl.
2. Place all other ingredients in saucepan and bring to boil, then reduce heat and simmer 2 minutes.
3. Pour pickling liquid over carrots and cool, uncovered. Chill carrots, covered, at least 1 day for flavors to develop.

If refrigerated the carrots will keep for up to 1 month

{**preparation time** 35 minutes **makes** 1 jar}

Lawnies Pickled Eggs

12 large eggs
4 cups white vinegar
7 cloves garlic
1 ½ tablespoon peppercorns
1 tablespoon allspice
2 slices ginger

1. Place eggs in saucepan and cover with water. Bring to boil. Cover, remove from heat, and let eggs sit in hot water for 10 to 12 minutes. Cool in cold water and peel.
2. In a saucepan, combine vinegar, garlic, peppercorns and allspice. Add sliced ginger if desired. Simmer for 10 minutes.
3. Place eggs in sterilized preserving jars. Pour vinegar mixture over eggs.
4. Seal and immerse jars in a large saucepan with a wire rack to hold jars at least 1-inch water above tops of jars. Cover and boil for 10 minutes. Remove jars and cool. Check seals, the lid should not move at all when pressed.
5. Store eggs for about one month before opening.

{**preparation time** 45 minutes **makes** 12 eggs}

Old Fashioned Pickled Eggplant

5 cups diced eggplant (peeled)
1 tablespoon salt
1 cup white wine vinegar
1 teaspoon chili flakes
1 ¼ cups extra-virgin olive oil
1 red bell pepper
7 garlic cloves (minced)
1 ½ tablespoon dried oregano

1. Combine eggplant and salt in a large bowl. Place another bowl on top of the eggplant and weigh it down with a clean rock or some canned food , allow it to sit for 2 an hour and a half.
2. Transfer eggplant to a fine mesh strainer and rinse off the salt under cold running water. Press out any excess water, spread the eggplant in a single layer on a baking sheet, and pat dry with paper towels.
3. Combine vinegar and red chili flakes in a pot and bring to a boil over medium-high heat.
4. Add eggplant and simmer for 2 minutes. Remove from heat and let eggplant stand in vinegar for 10 minutes.
5. Add remaining ingredients and stir to combine. Transfer to a clean sterilized jar. Let cool to room temperature, cover, and refrigerate at least 3 days before serving.

{preparation time 80 minutes makes 1 jar}

Pickled Nectarines

6 large nectarines
2 cups white vinegar
¾ white sugar
2 teaspoon salt
3 star anise
3 cinnamon sticks
3 bay leaves
¾ teaspoon black peppercorns
¾ teaspoon red pepper flakes

1. Wash nectarines and slice into 12 wedges per piece of fruit.
2. In a pot, combine 2 cups of white vinegar with 2 cups water, 3/4 cup granulated white sugar and 2 teaspoons salt and bring to boil over medium high heat. Once the liquid boils add the sliced nectarines and stir in until all slices are covered with the brine.
3. Simmer gently for 3 minutes and remove pot from heat.
4. Divide the spices evenly between 3 jars
5. Carefully ladle the fruit into the jars, using a wooden spoon handle to help the nectarine slices settle into place.
6. Pour brine over the nectarines to cover.
7. Tap jars gently to help dislodge any air bubbles that may be trapped between the nectarine slices.
8. Place the lids on the jar. Allow the jars to cool completely before putting them in the fridge.
9. If processing for shelf stability, carefully lower jars into boiling water bath and process for 10 minutes.
10. Pickled nectarines can be eaten as soon as cooled but will taste better if you allow them to sit in the jars for at least 48 hours before eating.

{**preparation time** 20 minutes **makes** 3 jars}

Classic Spiced Pears

8 crisp pears
4 cups white wine vinegar
zest of one lemon (strips)
2 cups white sugar
2 cups water
7 cloves
1 cinnamon stick
1 tablespoon thin sliced ginger
¾ teaspoon black peppercorns
½ teaspoon all spice berries

1. Combine all ingredients except for the pears in to a pot and bring to the boil, stirring until all the sugar is dissolved
2. Peel and core the pears
3. Cut the pears in to quarters and add them to the pot, simmer for 1 minute
4. Remove the pears and pack them in to sterilized jars.
5. Pour the vinegar mixture over the pears and seal the jars.
6. Store refrigerated or in a cool dark place and these pears will keep for up to 12 months

{**preparation time** 20 minutes **makes** 2 jars}

Green Tomato Pickles

5 ½ kg green tomatoes
2 ½ kg white onions
140 grams salt
2 tablespoon water
1 ½ kg sugar
1 bottle of Ezy Sauce
1 tablespoon mustard powder
1 tablespoon curry powder
1 tablespoon corn flour
2 teaspoons turmeric powder

1. Slice into a large dish the green tomatoes and onions.
2. Mix the salt in with the tomato and onions, cover and leave to stand for 12 hours.
3. After that time, add mustard, curry, corn flour, turmeric and water to a small mixing bowl and mix to make a runny paste. Set this aside for later
4. Place the onion and tomato mix into a large boiler and bring to the boil
5. Once boiling add the sugar and Ezy Sauce. Boil until thick (at least an hour).
6. Add the runny spice mix and cook for a further half hour stirring occasionally.
7. Once set remove from heat and bottle in clean sterilized glass jars.

Can't find Ezy sauce? Make your own version:

30g (1oz) mace
30g (1oz) cloves
30g (1oz) allspice
15g (½ oz) chilies
30g (1oz) pepper
60g (2oz) ginger

Combine all ingredients together to make the sauce.

{**preparation + cook time** 2 hours **makes** 8 jars}

Pickled Cauliflower and Onions

1 medium cauliflower
3 onions
1 medium red bell pepper
1 tablespoon salt
1 cup white vinegar
½ cup white sugar
½ teaspoon ground allspice
2 whole cloves
1 teaspoon turmeric
1 tablespoon plain flour
1 bay leaf
1 tablespoon curry powder
1 tablespoon dry mustard
1 tablespoon seeded mustard
¼ cup white vinegar, extra

1. Cut the cauliflower into small flowerets,
2. Dice the onions and capsicum into similar sized pieces. Place all vegetables and salt in a large bowl and them mix gently. Cover with cling film and stand overnight.
3. The following day rinse vegetables well under cold water ensure you remove any excess.
4. Combine the vinegar, sugar, allspice, cloves and bay leaf in large saucepan and bring to the boil.
5. Once boiling add vegetables and cover the pot with foil and let simmer for about 20 minutes or until vegetables are just tender; stir occasionally.
6. Blend remaining ingredients in bowl with extra vinegar, stir into vegetable mixture, stir constantly over heat until mixture boils and thickens.
7. Pour into hot sterilized jars; seal when the mixture is cold

{preparation + cook time 1 hour makes 2 jars}

Fancy-Schmancy Artichoke Heart Pickle

Suggested Jar: Regular Mouth, half-pint

1 lb artichoke hearts,
8 cloves garlic, peeled
1-3/4 cups red wine vinegar
1 cups water
1 tbsp sugar
2 tbsp salt

1. Wash and sterilize bottles
2. Slice artichoke hearts into ⅛ pieces.
3. In a medium-sized pot, combine vinegar, water, sugar and salt, bring to boil and cook for five minutes.
4. Place 2 cloves garlic in each jar.
5. Add artichoke hearts to jars and top with vinegar mixture leaving 1/2" headspace.
6. Process and allow to pickle for five days before opening jars.

{preparation + cook time 1 hour makes 4 half pint jars}

Artichoke Carrot Pickle

Suggested Jar: Regular Mouth, half-pint

1 lb artichoke hearts
1/2 lb carrots, peeled and sliced
1 tbsp sugar
1 tbsp pickling salt
1 cup filtered water
1 cup red wine vinegar

1. Thoroughly wash jars and lids with soap and water, sterilize in dishwasher or water bath.
2. Quarter artichoke hearts.
3. Bring water, vinegar, salt and sugar to a boil.
4. Pack hearts and carrots into jars.
5. Make sure there are no air bubbles, seal and place in fridge for 24 hours before opening.

{**preparation + cook time** 30 mins **makes** 3 pint jars}

Carolina's Pickled Cukes

Suggested Jar: Regular Mouth, Quart

8-10 lbs Kirby cucumbers
18 cloves garlic, peeled
18 peppercorns
6 cups distilled white vinegar or cider vinegar
6 cups water
1 cup and 1 tbsp pickling salt
1 tablespoon sugar

1. Wash and dry cucumbers, in order to ensure the crispest pickle chop off bottom ends.
2. In a large dish, layer cucumbers and 1 cup salt.
3. Place heavy dish over the cucumbers so they are weighed down in order to drain water and leave for 12 hours.
4. Thoroughly wash canning jars with soap and water and sterilize.
5. For the pickles, bring salt, sugar, water and vinegar to boil.
6. Carefully remove jars from water using canning tongs.
7. Place 4 peppercorns, 3 cloves garlic in each jar.
8. Divide cucumbers into each of the jars and pour water mixture into jars, leaving a 1/4" space at the top.
9. Place jars back in water canner and bring water to a boil, allowing jars to sit in boiling water for 15 minutes.
10. Give pickles a week to develop flavours before opening.

{**preparation + cook time** 1 hour **makes** 6 quarts}

Barnyard Beetroot Pickles

Suggested Jar: Regular Mouth, Pint

2 lbs beetroot
1 cup pickling salt
2 cups water
2 cups vinegar
1 cup sugar
4 cloves
4 glass pint jars

1. Wash and sterilize pickling jars.
2. Peel and chop beetroot into 1" slices.
3. Cook beetroot in boiling water, set aside.
4. In a separate pot, bring remaining ingredients to a boil.
5. Place beetroot in jars, top with sugar mixture, leaving ½" at top.
6. Place jars in water bath for processing.
7. Remove jars using canning tongs and allow to ferment for one week.

{**preparation + cook time** 1 hour **makes** 4 pint jars}

Minty Blueberry Pickle

Suggested Jar: Regular Mouth, half-pint

2 lbs blueberries
1 small red onion, peeled and sliced
1/2 cup mint
1 cup cider vinegar
1 cup water
2 tbsp sea salt
2 tbsp cane sugar

1. Wash and sterilize jars.
2. Bring water, vinegar, salt and sugar to a boil and continue to cook for 5 minutes.
3. Place berries, mint and onion in jars.
4. Add vinegar mixture to jars leaving 1/2" headspace.
5. Seal jars, process and refrigerate after opening.

{preparation + cook time 30 mins makes 2 pint jars}

Bert's Beet and Cauliflower Pickle

Suggested Jar: Wide-mouth quart jar

1 cup red beets, steamed
4 cups cauliflower florets
3 cloves garlic, peeled
1 cup cider vinegar
1 cup water
2 sprigs dill
2 tbsp sea salt

1. In medium-sized pot combine vinegar, water, beets and salt, bring to boil and cook for 10 minutes.
2. Place garlic and dill in jar, pack in cauliflower.
3. Top with beet and vinegar mixture, leaving 1/2" headspace.
4. Process in water bath and pickle for 48 hours before opening.

{**preparation + cook time** 30 mins **makes** 1 quart}

Brussel Sprout Pickle

Suggested Jar: Wide-mouth pint

2 lbs Brussels sprouts
8 garlic cloves, peeled
8 peppercorns
1 tsp oregano
4 cloves
3 cups distilled vinegar
2 cups water
2 tbsp sugar

1. Wash and sterilize bottles
2. In a medium-sized pot, combine vinegar, water, sugar, oregano, cloves and bring to boil.
3. Place 2 garlic cloves and 2 peppercorns in each jar.
4. Pack Brussels sprouts into jar and add vinegar mixture, leaving 1/2" headspace.
5. Process and store for 1 week before opening.

{**preparation + cook time** 1 hour **makes** 4 pints}

Green Bean Pickle

Suggested Jar: Regular Mouth pint

2 lbs green beans, ends snipped
1 carrot, peeled and sliced
12 garlic cloves, peeled
12 peppercorns
3 cups distilled vinegar
2 cups water
1 tbsp sugar

1. Wash and sterilize bottles
2. In a medium-sized pot, combine vinegar, water, sugar and bring to boil.
3. Place 3 garlic cloves and 3 peppercorns in each jar.
4. Pack beans into jar and pour in vinegar mixture leaving 1/2" headspace.
5. Process and shelve for 1 week before opening

{**preparation + cook time** 1 hour **makes** 4 pints}

Festive Bell Pepper Pickle

Suggested Jar: Regular Mouth, Quart

4 lbs green bell pepper, julienned
4 lbs red bell pepper, julienned
6 cups vinegar
6 cups water
1 cup pickling salt
16 cloves garlic, peeled

1. Wash glass jars with soap and water, fill with water and sterilize.
2. In separate pot bring salt, water, vinegar to boil.
3. Combine bell peppers.
4. Pack bell peppers in each jar, top with 4 cloves garlic.
5. Pour vinegar mixture into each jar, leaving ½" head space.
6. Close up jars, process and allow flavours to develop for five days before opening.

{**preparation + cook time** 30 mins **makes** 6 quarts}

Cabbage Patch Pickle

Suggested Jar: Regular Mouth, Quart

8 lbs cabbage, coarsely chopped
6 carrots, peeled and sliced
2 red bell pepper, julienned
6 cups vinegar
6 cups water
1 cup pickling salt
20 cloves garlic, peeled
6 tsp fresh dill

1. Wash glass jars with soap and water, sterilize.
2. In separate pot bring salt, water, vinegar and four garlic cloves to boil.
3. Mix raw cabbage, carrots and red bell peppers.
4. Pack in a mixture of veggies in each jar, top with tsp dill and 4 cloves garlic.
5. Pour vinegar mixture into each jar, leaving ½" space at the top.
6. Seal jars and process.

Allow to rest for one week before opening readied pickles

{preparation + cook time 1 hour makes 6 quarts}

Red Cabbage and Bell Pepper Pickle

Suggested Jar: Wide Mouth, Quart

6 lbs red cabbage, coarsely chopped
2 lbs red bell peppers, seeded, julienned
16 peppercorns
6 cups vinegar
6 cups water
1 cup pickling salt
16 cloves garlic, peeled
6 tsp fresh dill

1. Wash glass jars with soap and water and sterilize.
2. In separate pot bring water, vinegar and four garlic cloves to boil.
3. Combine cabbage and bell peppers.
4. Pack veggies in each jar, top with 1 tsp dill and 4 cloves garlic.
5. Pour vinegar mixture into each jar, leaving 1/4" headspace.
6. Close up jars and process.
7. Remove and allow flavours to combine for five days before opening jars.

{**preparation + cook time** 1 hour **makes** 6 quarts}

Sweet Carolina's Carrot Ginger Pickle

Suggested Jar: Regular Mouth, Pint

1 lb carrot
4 tsp ginger, chopped
1 tsp ground cumin
1 tbsp sugar
1 tbsp pickling salt
1 cup filtered water
1 cup vinegar
2 tbsp olive oil

1. Wash and sterilize jars.
2. Peel and slice carrots into short sticks.
3. Heat olive oil, add cumin and carrot sticks.
4. Add water, vinegar, salt and sugar, bringing to a boil.
5. Allow carrots to cook for a few minutes so they are slightly tender but still fairly crisp.
6. Place 1 tsp fresh ginger in each jar and top with carrot mixture.
7. Make sure there are no air bubbles, seal and place in fridge, will be good for up to one month

{**preparation + cook time** 1 hour **makes** 4 ½ pints}

Carrot Raisin Pickle

Suggested Jar: Regular Mouth, Pint

2 lbs carrots, peeled and sliced
1 cup raisins
4 red chilli peppers
3 cups distilled vinegar
2 cups water
1 tbsp sugar
2 tbsp salt

1. Wash and sterilize bottles
2. In a medium-sized pot, combine vinegar, water, sugar and salt, bring to boil.
3. Place 1/4 cup raisin and 1 chilli pepper in each jar.
4. Add carrots to jars and top with vinegar mixture, leaving 1/2" headspace.
5. Process and allow to pickle for five days before opening jar.

{preparation + cook time 1 hour makes 4 pints}

Quick'n Easy Veg out Pickle

Suggested Jar: Wide Mouth, Quart

4 cups cauliflower florets
2 lbs cucumbers, sliced
2 lbs carrots, sliced
12 peppercorns
14 cloves garlic, peeled
8 cups water
2 cups red wine vinegar
4 cups distilled vinegar
3 tbsp sea salt
1 tbsp sugar
6 sprigs fresh dill

1. Wash and sterilize bottles
2. Place water, vinegars, 2 garlic cloves, salt and sugar in a large pot, bring to a rolling boil and continue to cook for 10 minutes.
3. Place sprig of dill, 2 peppercorns and 2 garlic cloves in the bottom of each jar and stuff with combination of veggies.
4. Pour liquid over top while leaving 1/4" headspace.
5. Allow to cool for 12 hours.
6. Refrigerate and use within 3 months.

{preparation + cook time 1 hour makes 6 quarts}

The Busy Supermom Pickle

Suggested Jar: Regular Mouth, Quart

8 lbs Kirby cucumbers, sliced
18 peppercorns
18 coriander seeds
12 cloves garlic, peeled
7 cups water
6 cups distilled vinegar
2 tbsp sea salt
2 tbsp cane sugar

1. Wash and sterilize bottles
2. Place water, vinegars, 2 garlic cloves in a large pot, bring to a rolling boil and continue to cook for 10 minutes.
3. Place sprig of 3 peppercorns, 3 coriander seeds and 2 garlic cloves in the bottom of each jar and stuff with combination of veggies.
4. Pour liquid over top while leaving 1/4" headspace.
5. Allow to cool for 12 hours.
6. Refrigerate and use within 3 months.

{preparation + cook time 1 hour makes 6 quarts}

Easy Peazy Freezer Pickle

Suggested Jar: Freezer-Friendly Container

6 cups Kirby pickles, ends removed
1 red bell pepper, seeded and julienned
1 onion, peeled and chopped
1 tsp celery seed
1 cup distilled vinegar
1 cup sugar
2 tbsp salt

1. Place saucepan over low-heat, add sugar, vinegar, salt and mix until sugar is dissolved.
2. Mix vinegar mixture and cucumbers in a glass bowl and refrigerate for 12 hours.
3. Place in freezer-friendly container(s) and freeze until use.

{preparation + cook time 30 mins **makes** 3 pints}

Cauliflower Mustard Pickles

Suggested Jar: Regular Mouth, Quart

10 cups cauliflower florets
2 large carrots, peeled and sliced
14 mustard seeds
10 cloves garlic, peeled
6 cups water
3 cups red wine vinegar
2 tbsp sea salt
1 tbsp sugar

1. Wash and sterilize bottles
2. Place water, vinegars, 2 garlic cloves and 2 mustard seeds in a large pot, bring to a rolling boil and continue to cook for 5 minutes.
3. Place 2 mustard seeds and 2 garlic cloves in the bottom of each jar and stuff with combination of veggies.
4. Pour liquid over top while leaving 1/4" headspace.
5. Allow to cool for 12 hours.
6. Refrigerate and use within 3 months.

{**preparation + cook time** 30 mins **makes** 4 quarts}

Corn Freezer Pickle

Suggested Jar: Freezer-Friendly Container

6 cups corn kernels
1 red bell pepper, seeded and chopped
6 peppercorns
3 sprigs dill
1 cup red wine vinegar
3/4 cup water
1/2 cup sugar
2 tbsp salt

1. Place saucepan over low-heat, add sugar, vinegar, water, salt and mix until sugar is dissolved.
2. Mix remaining ingredients with vinegar mixture in a glass bowl and refrigerate for 12 hours.
3. Place in freezer-friendly container(s) and freeze until use.

{preparation + cook time 30 mins makes 3 pints}

Purple Egg Pickle

Suggested Jar: Wide Mouth, Quart

1 cup red beets, steamed
10 eggs
1 cup red wine vinegar
1 cup water
2 peppercorns
2 sprigs dill
2 tbsp sea salt

1. Hard-boil eggs, peel, set aside.
2. In medium-sized pot combine vinegar, water, beets and salt, bring to boil and cook for 10 minutes.
3. Place dill and peppercorn in jar, add eggs.
4. Pour vinegar mixture in jar, leaving 1/2" headspace.
5. Cool for 12 hours and refrigerate for 24 hours before opening jar.

{**preparation + cook time** 40 mins **makes** 1 quart}

Garlic Eggplant Pickle

Suggested Jar: Regular Mouth, Pint

4 lbs eggplant
18 cloves garlic, peeled
3-½ cups vinegar
3 cups water
3 tbsp pickling salt
3 tbsp sugar
olive oil

1. Wash and sterilize jars
2. Preheat broiler and lightly coat roasting pan with olive oil
3. Place eggplant in pan and roast for 15 minutes.
4. Remove from oven, cut off tops and cut into strips (leave skin on).
5. In a separate pot, bring water, vinegar, salt and sugar to boil.
6. Place three cloves garlic in each pint jar, pack in eggplant and pour vinegar mixture over top.
7. Process in water bath and store for five days before opening.

{preparation + cook time 40 mins **makes 6 pints**}

Aunty Alsa's Ginger Pickle

Suggested Jar: Regular Mouth, Pint

1 lb ginger, peeled and chopped
1 tsp ground coriander
1 green chili pepper, deseeded and chopped
1 tbsp pickling salt
1 cup filtered water
1 cup malt vinegar

1. Wash and sterilize jars.
2. Peel and slice ginger into short sticks.
3. Bring water, vinegar, salt, coriander and chili pepper to boil.
4. Place fresh ginger in each jar and top with vinegar mixture.
5. Make sure there are no air bubbles, seal and place in fridge, will be good for up to two months.

{**preparation + cook time** 30 mins **makes** 4 ½ pints}

Spicy Jalapeno Pickle

Suggested Jar: Regular Mouth, Pint

1 lb jalapenos
4 cloves garlic, peeled
1 cup white wine vinegar
1 cup water
2 tbsp sea salt
1 tbsp sugar

1. Thoroughly wash jars and lids and sterilize using dishwasher or canning pot method. .
2. Slice jalapenos ½" think and discard seeds if you do not want a high-heat pickle.
3. Bring water, vinegar, salt and sugar to a boil.
4. Pack jalapenos into jars.
5. Make sure there are no air bubbles, seal and place in fridge for four days before opening.

{**preparation + cook time** 30 mins **makes** 2 pints}

Mad Dawg's Mushroom Farm Pickle

Suggested Jar: Regular Mouth, Pint

4 lbs mushrooms, cleaned and sliced
14 cloves garlic, peeled
3 cups vinegar
3 cups water
3 tbsp pickling salt
1 tbsp sugar

1. Wash and sterilize jars
2. Bring water, vinegar, salt, sugar and two cloves garlic to boil in a large pot.
3. Pack mushrooms in jar and top with 2 cloves garlic per pint jar.
4. Pour vinegar mixture over top.
5. Process in water bath and store for five days before opening.

{**preparation + cook time** 30 mins **makes** 6 pints}

Grandma's Okra Pickle

Suggested Jar: Regular Mouth, Pint

3 lbs okra
6 cloves garlic, peeled
6 green chilies
3-½ cups vinegar
3 cups water
3 tbsp pickling salt
1 tbsp sugar

1. Wash and sterilize jars
2. Bring large pot of water to boil, add okra and boil for five minutes.
3. Place okra in a pot of cold water to stop cooking process.
4. In a separate pot, bring water, vinegar, salt and sugar to boil.
5. Place one clove garlic and one chili pepper in bottom of each jar.
6. Pack jars with okra, pour vinegar mixture over top.
7. Process in water bath and store for five days before opening.

{preparation + cook time 30 mins **makes** 6 pints}

The put it on everything Onion Pickle

Suggested Jar: Regular Mouth, Quart

2 lbs onion peeled and sliced
2 limes, seeded and quartered
8 peppercorns
3 cups distilled vinegar
2 cups water
1 tbsp sugar
2 tbsp salt

1. Wash and sterilize bottles
2. In a medium-sized pot, combine vinegar, water, sugar and salt, bring to boil.
3. Place 4 peppercorns and 1 quartered lime in each jar.
4. Add onions to jars and top with vinegar mixture leaving 1/2" headspace.
5. Process and allow to develop for 48 hours before opening jar.

{**preparation + cook time** 30 mins **makes** 2 quarts}

The peachy keen Banana Pepper Pickle

Suggested Jar: Regular Mouth, Pint

2 lbs banana peppers, seeded
3 peaches
3 cups water
3 cups red wine vinegar
2 tbsp sea salt
1 tbsp sugar

1. Wash and sterilize jars.
2. Fill medium-sized pot with water and bring to boil.
3. Dunk peaches in water for 20 seconds, remove and peel.
4. Seed and slice peaches.
5. Chop peppers into rings.
6. Place water, vinegar, salt and sugar in large pot and bring to a boil.
7. Stuff peppers and peaches into jars
8. Fill jars with vinegar liquid, leaving 1/2" head space.
9. Process in water bath, store in cool place for 1 week before opening.

{preparation + cook time 40 mins **makes** 6 pints}

Roasted Red Pepper Pickle

Suggested Jar: Regular Mouth, Pint

3 lbs red bell pepper, seeded
12 cloves garlic, peeled
3-½ cups vinegar
3 cups water
3 tbsp pickling salt
3 tbsp sugar
olive oil

1. Wash and sterilize jars
2. Preheat broiler and lightly coat roasting pan with olive oil
3. Place seeded bell peppers in roasting pan and place in oven for 15 minutes.
4. Remove from oven and do a loose julienne.
5. In a separate pot, bring water, vinegar, salt and sugar to boil.
6. Place two cloves garlic in each pint jar, pack in red peppers and pour vinegar mixture over top.
7. Process in water bath and store for five days before opening.

{**preparation + cook time** 1 hour **makes** 6 pints}

Pickled Banana Peppers

Suggested Jar: Regular Mouth, Quart

8 lbs banana peppers, seeded, tops removed
6 cups vinegar
6 cups water
1 cup pickling salt
16 cloves garlic, peeled
6 tsp fresh dill

1. Wash glass jars with soap and water and sterilize jars.
2. In separate pot bring water, vinegar and four garlic cloves to boil.
3. Pack tomatillos in each jar, top with 1 tsp dill and 4 cloves garlic.
4. Pour vinegar mixture into each jar, leaving ½" head space.
5. Process jars in water bath.
6. Remove and allow flavours to combine for five days before opening jars.

{**preparation + cook time** 30 mins **makes** 6 quarts}

Radish Peppercorn Pickle

Suggested Jar: Regular Mouth, Pint

3 lbs radish, peeled and sliced
24 peppercorns
3-½ cups vinegar
3 cups water
3 tbsp pickling salt
1 tbsp sugar

1. Wash and sterilize jars
2. Bring large pot of water to boil, add carrots and boil for five minutes.
3. Place carrots in a pot of cold water to stop cooking process.
4. In a separate pot, bring water, vinegar, salt and sugar to boil.
5. Place 1 tsp ginger in each pint jar.
6. Pack jars with carrots, pour vinegar mixture over top.
7. Process in water bath and store for five days before opening.

{preparation + cook time 30 mins makes 6 pints}

Strawberry Onion Pickle

Suggested Jar: Regular Mouth, Pint

2 lbs strawberries
1 small red onion, peeled and sliced
4 peppercorns
1 cup red wine vinegar
1 cup water
2 tbsp sea salt
2 tbsp cane sugar

1. Wash and sterilize jars.
2. Bring water, vinegar, salt and sugar to a boil and continue to cook for 5 minutes.
3. Place 2 peppercorns in each jar.
4. Pack strawberries and onions into jars and fill with vinegar mixture.
5. Add vinegar mixture to jars leaving 1/2" headspace.
6. Seal jars and refrigerate for 24 hours before opening.

{**preparation + cook time** 30 mins **makes** 2 pints}

Pickled Green Tomatoes

Suggested Jar: Wide Mouth, Quart

8-10 lbs green tomatoes
18 cloves garlic, peeled
6 cups cider vinegar
6 cups water
1 cup and 1 tbsp pickling salt
1 tablespoon sugar

1. Wash, dry and slice tomatoes into ½" thick discs. .
2. In a large dish, layer green tomatoes and 1 cup salt.
3. Place heavy dish over the cucumbers so they are weighed down in order to drain water and leave for 12 hours.
4. Thoroughly wash canning jars with soap and water and sterilize in water bath.
5. For the pickles, bring salt, sugar, water and vinegar to boil, set aside.
6. Place 3 cloves garlic in each jar.
7. Divide green tomatoes evenly among six jars and pour water mixture into jars, leaving 1/2" headspace.
8. Process jars in water bath and store.
9. Give pickles a week to develop before partaking.

{**preparation + cook time** 1 hour **makes** 6 quarts}

Cherry Tomato Pickle

Suggested Jar: Regular Mouth, Pint

2 lb cherry tomatoes
4 basil leaves
4 tsp dill
2 tbsp sugar
2 tbsp pickling salt
2 cup filtered water
2 cup red wine vinegar

1. Thoroughly wash jars and lids with soap and water, sterilize in dishwasher or in pot of boiling water.
2. Bring water, vinegar, salt and sugar to a boil.
3. Evenly divide tomatoes among jars.
4. Make sure there are no air bubbles, seal and place in fridge for 24 hours before opening.
5. Tomatoes should be consumed within 1 month.

{**preparation + cook time** 30 mins **makes** 4 pints}

Texas Tomatillo Pickle

Suggested Jar: Regular Mouth, Quart

8 lbs tomatillos, washed and quartered
6 cups vinegar
6 cups water
1 cup pickling salt
16 cloves garlic, peeled
6 tsp fresh dill

1. Wash glass jars with soap and water and sterilize in water bath or dishwasher.
2. In separate pot bring water, vinegar and four garlic cloves to boil.
3. Pack tomatillos in each jar, top with 1 tsp dill and 4 cloves garlic.
4. Pour vinegar mixture into each jar, leaving ½" head space.
5. Close up bands, lids and process jars.
6. Remove and store for five days before opening up jars.

{**preparation + cook time** 30 mins **makes** 6 quarts}

Tomato Toss Pickle

Suggested Jar: Regular Mouth, Quart

8 lbs tomatoes, washed and quartered
6 cups vinegar
6 cups water
1 cup pickling salt
16 cloves garlic, peeled
3 tbsp oregano
6 bay leaves

1. Wash glass jars with soap and water and sterilize.
2. In separate pot bring water, vinegar and four garlic cloves to boil.
3. Combine bell peppers.
4. Pack tomatillos in each jar, top with 1 tsp dill and 4 cloves garlic.
5. Pour vinegar mixture into each jar, leaving ½" head space.
6. Close up jars, process in water bath for 15 minutes.
7. Remove and allow flavours to combine for seven days before opening jars.

{preparation + cook time 40 mins makes 6 quarts}

Hot Tomato Pickle

Suggested Jar: Regular Mouth, Pint

2 lbs cherry tomatoes
6 habanero peppers
6 cloves garlic, peeled
6 basil leaves
3 cups water
3 cups red wine vinegar
2 tbsp sea salt
1 tbsp sugar

1. Wash and sterilize jars.
2. Place water, vinegar, salt and sugar in large pot and bring to a boil.
3. Place 1 clove garlic, 1 habanero and 1 basil leaf in each jar.
4. Fill jars with vinegar liquid, leaving 1/2" head space.
5. Process in water bath, store in cool place for 1 week before opening.

{**preparation + cook time** 30 mins **makes** 6 pints}

Summer Fair Vege Pickle

Suggested Jar: Regular Mouth, Quart

3 lbs carrots, peeled, sliced
3 lbs cauliflower, chopped
2 lbs green beans
6 cups vinegar
6 cups water
1 cup pickling salt
16 cloves garlic, peeled
6 tsp fresh dill

1. Wash glass jars with soap and water and sterilize.
2. In separate pot bring water, vinegar and four garlic cloves to boil.
3. Pack in a mixture of veggies in each jar, top with tsp dill and 3 cloves garlic.
4. Pour vinegar mixture into each jar, leaving ½" space at the top.
5. Close jars with bands and lids, process in water bath.
6. Allow to rest for one week before opening readied pickles.

{preparation + cook time 40 mins makes 6 quarts}

Zucchini Ginger Pickle

Suggested Jar: Regular Mouth, Pint

3 lbs zucchinis, peeled and chopped into sticks
6 tbsp fresh ginger, chopped
3-½ cups vinegar
3 cups water
3 tbsp pickling salt
1 tbsp sugar

1. Wash and sterilize jars
2. In a separate pot, bring water, vinegar, salt and sugar to boil.
3. Place 1 tsp ginger in each pint jar.
4. Pack jars with zucchini, pour vinegar mixture over top.
5. Process in water bath and store for five days before opening.

{**preparation + cook time** 30 mins **makes** 6 pints}

Farmhouse Chutneys and Relishes

Chutneys are a relish which are usually made from sweet and tart or savory spices, a combination of more different fruits and vegetables which are chopped, but generally not pureed smooth. Perfect to use as a condiment next to meats or vegetable dishes.

A Relish is a pickled condiment usually made up of chopped vegetables or fruit, vinegar, sugar and spices

Harpers Tomato Relish

1 onion, finely chopped
2 garlic cloves, crushed
1 Teaspoon Chili Paste
500g dice tomatoes
1 tbs olive oil
1 tbs brown sugar

1. In a saucepan on medium heat, add the oil and cook the onions until soft. Add the garlic and chili paste and mix through
2. Add in the chopped tomatoes and cook and for 5 minutes stirring occasionally until the tomato breaks down.
3. Add the sugar and cook for 10 minutes or until the mixture thickens.
4. Set aside to cool

{**preparation + cook time** 30 minutes **makes** 2 jars}

Harpers BBQ Mushroom Relish

1tsp oil
2 onions, chopped
100g/4oz mushrooms, sliced
1 apple, cored and grated
600ml/ 1 pint water
1 cup tomato ketchup
2 tablespoons Worcestershire sauce
4 tablespoons English mustard

1. Heat oil in a pan and cook the onion and mushrooms until softened (about 3 minutes).
2. Add the apple, water, tomato ketchup, Worcestershire sauce and the English mustard. Cook for 10-15 minutes until thickened, stirring occasionally

{preparation + cook time 20 minutes makes 1 jars}

Fig Tomato & Caramelized Onion Relish

1 tablespoons olive oil
4 medium onions
2 tablespoons white wine vinegar
¼ cup sugar
6 large tomatoes, peeled and chopped
2 apples, peeled and chopped
3 ½ cups dried figs, sliced
½ cup lemon juice
4 cups sugar

1. Add the oil to a frying pan and fry onions until soft, then caramelize with the vinegar and 1/4 cup sugar until medium brown.
2. Combine tomato, apple and figs in a saucepan and simmer until soft.
3. Add the caramelized onions and the rest of the sugar. Heat gently until the sugar is dissolved, then bring it to a boil until it sets (about 15 minutes).
4. Allow to cool slightly then bottle and seal.

{preparation + cook time 30 minutes makes 3 jars}

Apple and Fig Chutney

12 medium figs, coarsely chopped
1 large onion, finely chopped
3 medium apples, peeled and finely chopped
½ cup finely chopped dried apricots
2 cups brown sugar
2 cups white vinegar
1 cup dry white wine
1 cup sultanas
¼ cup tomato paste
1 clove garlic
2 teaspoon mustard seeds
½ teaspoon ground cardamom
½ teaspoon ground cinnamon

1. Brown off the onions in a frying pan until soft
2. Add the figs, apples, apricots and brown sugar and heat until caramelized.
3. Once caramelized add all other ingredients and bring to the boil for 3 minutes
4. Reduce heat and simmer until thick
5. Allow to cool slightly then bottle and seal

{preparation + cook time 30 minutes makes 4 jars}

Roasted Pepper and Chili Tomato Relish

1.5kg ripe tomatoes
1kg red bell peppers
1 tablespoon olive oil
Pinch salt and pepper
8 red cayenne chili peppers
500g white onions, diced
2 teaspoons crushed garlic
1 cup brown sugar
1.5 cups malt vinegar
1 tablespoon curry powder
1 tablespoon mustard powder
1 teaspoon cayenne pepper (optional)
1 tablespoon corn flour

1. Preheat the oven to 200 Degrees Celsius
2. Slice the red bell peppers in half lengthways and remove the seeds.
3. Brush each half with Olive Oil and sprinkle with Salt and Pepper
4. Line a baking tray with baking paper and place the peppers sliced side up on the tray.
5. Roast the Peppers in the oven for 30 minutes, remove and allow to cool.
6. Dice the tomatoes and place in a large pot along with the onions
7. Add remaining ingredients (except the roasted peppers, chili's and corn flour) to the pot.
8. Bring the mixture to the boil, stirring well.
9. Reduce to a medium-low heat and cover with lid. Simmer for 20 minutes.
10. Peel and discard the skin from the roasted bell peppers. Dice them in to chunks and add to pot
11. Remove the lid and simmer on low heat until the mixture has reduced by almost half, stirring occasionally to prevent sticking to the pot.
12. Add a small amount of cold water to the corn flour and mix to create a runny paste.
13. Add corn flour to pot and simmer until thickened.

{preparation + cook time 60 minutes **makes** 6 jars}

Tomato Apple & Fig Relish

1 tablespoons olive oil
4 medium onions
2 tablespoons white wine vinegar
¼ cup sugar
6 large tomatoes, peeled and chopped
2 apples, peeled and chopped
3 ½ cups dried figs, sliced
½ cup lemon juice
4 cups sugar

1. Add the oil to a frying pan and fry onions until soft, then caramelize with the vinegar and ¼ cup sugar until medium brown.
2. Combine tomato, apple and figs in a saucepan and simmer until soft.
3. Add the caramelized onions and the rest of the sugar. Heat gently until the sugar is dissolved, then bring it to a boil until it sets (about 15 minutes).
4. Allow to cool slightly then bottle and seal.

{**preparation + cook time** 30 minutes **makes** 3 jars}

Caramelized Onion and Balsamic Chutney

8 red onions
1 table spoon of yellow mustard seeds
2 tbsp olive oil
250g brown sugar
175ml balsamic vinegar
175ml red wine vinegar

1. Slice the onions into short, thin slices and put them into a hot pan with the mustard seeds and oil. Cook the onions until brown and translucent
2. Add the sugar, the balsamic vinegar and the red wine vinegar, simmer for about 25 minutes until the chutney is thick and dark.
3. Allow to cool slightly before placing in to sterilized jars.
4. Can be consumed straight away however the longer you leave the chutney in the jar the deeper the flavors become.

{**preparation + cook time** 40 minutes **makes** 4 jars}

Balsamic Tomato Chutney

2kg ripe tomatoes, chopped
1kg ripe cherry tomatoes diced in quarters
4 red onions, roughly chopped
2 tbsp olive oil
175ml red wine vinegar
175ml balsamic vinegar
350g brown sugar
1tsp paprika
1tbsp dried oregano
¼ tsp cayenne pepper

1. Add the oil to a hot pan and brown the onions
2. Add the chopped tomatoes, red wine vinegar and seasoning. Cook down until thick.
3. In a small bowl, dissolve the sugar into the Balsamic vinegar and add to the pan.
4. Add the cherry tomatoes to the pan and stir well
5. Add the paprika, oregano and cayenne pepper.
6. Simmer on low heat until mixture thickens. Add salt and pepper to taste if required.
7. Allow to cool slightly then pour mixture in to sterilized jars.
8. Leave 1 week before consuming for a deeper flavor

{preparation + cook time 40 minutes makes 4 jars}

Dads Mustard Onion Relish

2 tablespoons olive oil
3 onions, peeled and sliced
1 teaspoon minced garlic
3 tablespoons brown sugar
4 tablespoons red wine vinegar
2 teaspoons whole grain mustard
salt and pepper, to taste

1. Add the oil to a hot pan and fry the onions until brown
2. Add the garlic and stir in to the onions
3. Add the sugar, vinegar and mustard.
4. Reduce heat and simmer until the mixture starts to thicken.
5. Season with salt and pepper to taste

{**preparation + cook time** 20 minutes **makes** 1 jars}

Alsa's Sweet Pickle Relish

4 cups cucumbers, deseeded and chopped
2 cups onions, chopped
1 cup green bell pepper, chopped
1 cup red bell pepper, chopped
¼ cup salt
1 ¾ cups sugar
1 tablespoon mustard seeds
1 cups cider vinegar
1 tablespoon celery seed

1. Deseed the cucumbers by slicing them in half-length ways and scooping out the seeds with a teaspoon.
2. Deseed the bell peppers and place them in a food processor along with the cucumbers. Process until finely chopped. Do not over process them or else you will end up with mush. If you don't have a food processor just finely chop them using a knife.
3. Put all the vegetables in a large bowl and sprinkle the salt over the top.
4. Cover with cold water and let stand for 2 hours.
5. Using a sieve drain out as much liquid as possible .
6. Combine the sugar, vinegar and mustard seeds in a large pot and bring it to boil.
7. Add the vegetables and bring back to boil then lower the heat and simmer for 10 minutes
8. Spoon the mixture in to jars and place the lids on
9. Place the jars in to a hot water bath for 10 minutes
10. Pickles taste best after 2 weeks in the jar but can be consumed straight away if you desire.

{**preparation + cook time** 20 minutes **makes** 1 jars}

Green Tomato Relish

8 chopped green tomatoes
1 large white onion, chopped
1 large green bell pepper, chopped
2 tablespoons salt
1 cup sugar
1 tablespoon yellow mustard
1 teaspoon celery salt
1 teaspoon ground cloves
1 cup vinegar

1. Combine tomatoes, onion, and pepper in large bowl and sprinkle the salt over the top then mix in gently.
2. Cover the vegetables and let stand for one hour
3. Using a sieve drain all the liquid off the vegetables
4. Combine drained vegetables, sugar, mustard, ground cloves and celery salt in a large pot.
5. Stir in vinegar and simmer for 20 minutes.
6. Transfer the hot relish mixture to sterilized jars and place the caps on the jars
7. Place the sealed jars in to a hot water bath for 10 minutes
8. The relish is best served after 2 weeks however can also be consumed straight away

{preparation + cook time 40 minutes makes 3 jars}

Corn Relish

1kg corn kernels
1 red bell pepper, de-seeded and chopped
2 chopped onions
¼ cup salt
2 cups white sugar
2 cups white vinegar
2 teaspoons mustard powder
2 teaspoons turmeric
2 tablespoons corn flour

1. Combine the corn, capsicum and onion in a non re-active bowl, add the salt and mix through Leave stand for two hours then drain using a colander.
2. Place the sugar, vinegar, drained vegetables, mustard and turmeric in a large saucepan. Bring to the boil and cook over a medium heat for 25 to 30 minutes.
3. Mix the corn flour with a small amount of water to form a runny paste, add it to the relish mixture to thicken it.
4. Remove from heat and transfer mixture in to clean sterilized jars. Seal the jars.

{**preparation + cook time** 45 minutes **makes** 3 jars}

Mango Chutney

7 mangoes
1 cup cider vinegar
1 ¼ cup packed light brown sugar
2 tablespoons minced garlic
1 2-inch fresh ginger, peeled and thinly sliced
1 teaspoon cayenne pepper
salt and freshly ground pepper

1. Peel and dice the mangos in to small pieces
2. Add the mangos, vinegar, sugar, garlic, ginger and cayenne pepper to a large pot and bring to boil over medium heat
3. Once boiling turn back the heat and allow it to simmer for 25 to 30 minutes, stirring occasionally.
4. Remove from heat and transfer chutney in to sterilized jars.
5. Place the lids on the jars and then place the jars in a hot water bath for 10 minutes

{preparation + cook time 45 minutes **makes** 3 jars}

Christmas Chutney

1kg tomatoes
3 red bell peppers
1 Eggplant
1 green bell pepper
700g onions, finely chopped
4 cloves garlic, crushed
350g white sugar
300ml white wine vinegar
1 tbsp salt
½ tsp cayenne pepper
1 tbsp coriander seeds, crushed
1 tbsp paprika

1. Peel the tomatoes
2. Chop the tomatoes and eggplant and seed and chop the bell peppers.
3. Put in a large heavy-based pan with the onions and garlic and cover with a lid, lower the heat and gently simmer for about one hour, stirring occasionally, until tender. Do not add any liquid, the vegetables will simmer in their own juices.
4. Add the sugar, vinegar, salt, coriander, paprika and cayenne into the pan and bring to the boil over a medium heat, stirring, until the sugar has dissolved. Continue to boil for 30 minutes or so, until the mixture achieves a chunky chutney consistency and the surplus watery liquid has evaporated. Take care towards the end of the cooking time to continue stirring so that the chutney doesn't catch on the bottom of the pan.
5. Ladle the chutney into sterilized jars. Seal the jars while still hot. Leave to mature for at least a month in a cool dark place.

{preparation + cook time 1 hour 45 minutes makes 5 jars}

Caramelised Onion and Apple Chutney

6 large red onions
2 tablespoons olive vegetable oil
3 apples
4 teaspoons crushed garlic
3 cups golden balsamic vinegar
3 cups brown sugar
3 bay leaves
20 crushed peppercorns
1 teaspoon ground cloves

1. Finely chop the onions and cook them in the oil in a large pot until soft.
2. Dice the apples in to medium sized chunks and add them to the pot, stir.
3. Add the garlic, vinegar, brown sugar, bay leaves, crushed peppercorns and ground cloves to the mixture and stir well
4. Bring the mixture to a boil and then down to a simmer. Continue to simmer until the onions are translucent and the liquid has nearly evaporated. This can take up to an hour or more.
5. Drag a wooden spoon through the mixture, across the bottom of the pan. If it leaves a clear path, with only a little liquid running back, then it's ready
6. Transfer in to sterilized jars and seal.
7. Can eat immediately or leave it for a few days to deepen the flavors.

{**preparation + cook time** 2 hours **makes** 2 jars}

Summer Fair Hickory Bacon Chutney

Suggested Jar: Wide Mouth, pint

1 lb hickory-smoked bacon
¼ cup bitter dark chocolate
½ cup cashews, chopped
1 red onion, peeled and chopped
1 cup brown sugar
1 cup red wine vinegar
1 tsp sea salt

1. Wash and sterilize jar and lid.
2. Cook bacon in skillet until brown, allow to cool, chop, set aside.
3. Bring vinegar to a boil, add remaining ingredients save bacon and cook for 10 minutes on medium heat.
4. Add bacon, reduce heat to low and simmer for 30 minutes.

Cool, spoon into jar, refrigerate and use within two weeks

{**preparation + cook time** 1 hour **makes** 1 pint jar}

Basil Pine Nut Chutney

Suggested Jar: Regular Mouth, Half Pint

3 cups fresh basil
1 red onion, peeled and diced
½ cup pine nuts
1 cup red wine vinegar
1 tsp sea salt
1/2 tsp paprika
¼ cup brown sugar

1. Wash jars and sterilize.
2. Place all items in blender, mix until smooth.
3. Place stockpot over medium heat, add blender content, cover and simmer for 30 minutes.
4. Pour into jars, cool, refrigerate and use within three weeks.

{**preparation + cook time** 1 hour **makes** 1 pints}

Apple Ginger Chutney

Suggested Jar: Regular Mouth, Pint

3 lbs apples, peeled and chopped
1 sweet onion, peeled and chopped
3 tsp grated ginger
1 cup brown sugar
1/2 cup raisins
1/2 tbsp sea salt
1 cup cider vinegar
1/2 tsp cinnamon
Olive oil

1. Heat 2 tbsp olive oil in large saucepan over medium heat.
2. Add onions, apples, cook until fragrant.
3. Add ginger and sugar, cook for two minutes and add remaining ingredients.
4. Bring to boil, reduce heat to low and allow to simmer for 45 minutes.
5. Pour into jars leaving ½" headspace and process.
6. Store for up to a year.

{preparation + cook time 1 hour **makes** 1 ½ quarts }

Banana Chutney

Suggested Jar: Regular Mouth, Half Pint

4 cups bananas, mashed
1 cup tomatoes, chopped
1/2 cup walnuts chopped
1 cup brown sugar
1 cup distilled vinegar
1 tsp salt

1. Wash and sterilize jar.
2. Place vinegar in large skillet and bring to boil.
3. Add sugar and stir for five minutes.
4. Add remaining ingredients and bring to a boil.
5. Reduce heat to low and cook for 30 minutes.
6. Cool.
7. Pour into jars leaving 1/2" headspace.
8. Process and store for up to 6 months

{**preparation + cook time** 1 hour **makes** 3 pints}

Minty Beetroot Chutney

Suggested Jar: Regular Mouth, Pint

3 lbs beetroot, peeled and sliced
1 onion, peeled and chopped
2 cloves garlic, peeled and chopped
1 cup fresh mint, chopped
1 cup brown sugar
1 tbsp sea salt
1 tsp paprika
1 cup red wine vinegar
Olive oil

1. Wash and sterilize canning jars.
2. Heat 2 tbsp olive oil in large saucepan over medium heat.
3. Add onions, beetroot and cook until fragrant.
4. Add mint and sugar, cook for two minutes and add remaining ingredients.
5. Bring to boil, reduce heat to low and allow to simmer for 45 minutes.
6. Pour into jars, seal and store for up to six months.

{**preparation + cook time** 1 hour **makes** 1 ½ quarts}

Blueberry Chutney

Suggested Jar: Regular Mouth, Half Pint

2 cups blueberries
1/2 cup almonds, chopped
1 onion, peeled and chopped
1/2 cup brown sugar
1 cup cider vinegar
1 tsp sea salt
1/2 tbsp crushed black pepper

1. Wash and sterilize jar.
2. Place red wine vinegar in large skillet and bring to boil.
3. Add sugar and stir for five minutes.
4. Add remaining ingredients and bring to a boil.
5. Reduce heat to low and cook for 30 minutes.
6. Pour into jars leaving 1/2" headspace.
7. Process and store for up to 6 months.

{preparation + cook time 1 hour makes 1 quart}

Carrot Raisin Chutney

Suggested Jar: Regular Mouth, Half Pint

3 cups carrots, shredded
1.5 cups red wine vinegar
1 red onion, peeled and diced
1/2 cup raisins
1 red chilli pepper
1/2 cup brown sugar
1 vanilla bean

1. Remove seeds from vanilla bean.
2. Bring vinegar to boil in saucepan, add ingredients (including beans. and pod)
3. Cook on medium heat for 10 minutes while stirring.
4. Reduce, simmer on low for 30 minutes.
5. Remove vanilla pod.
6. Cool, pour into jars leaving 1/2" headspace.
7. Process and store for up to a year.

{preparation + cook time 1 hour **makes** 1 ½ pints}

Cherry Chutney

Suggested Jar: Regular Mouth, Half Pint

3 cups cherries, pitted
1.5 cups red wine vinegar
1 sweet onion, peeled and chopped
1/2 cup dates, pitted and chopped
1 cinnamon stick
4 cloves

1. Wash and sterilize jars.
2. Place ingredients in saucepan and bring to a boil over medium heat.
3. Turn heat to low and allow to simmer for 45 minutes, stir occasionally.
4. Remove from heat, cool and pour into jars.
5. Process jars in water bath and store for up to 3 months.

{**preparation + cook time** 1.5 hours **makes** 1 ½ pints}

Fresh Coriander Chutney

Suggested Jar: Regular Mouth, Half Pint

3 cups fresh coriander
1 cup fresh mint
1/2 cup extra virgin olive oil
1/2 cup vinegar
1 tsp salt
1/2 tsp paprika
1/2 tsp cumin
1 tbsp sugar

1. Wash jars and sterilize.
2. Place all items in blender, mix until smooth.
3. Pour into jars, refrigerate and use within one week.

{**preparation + cook time** 20 mins **makes** 2 pints}

Green Chilli Chutney

Suggested Jar: Regular Mouth, Half Pint

1.5 cup green Chilli, roughly chopped
1 red onion, peeled and diced
1 cup parsley, washed and chopped
2 cups distilled vinegar
1 red chilli pepper
1/2 cup brown sugar

1. Place chilies, parsley and onions in blender and crush.
2. Bring vinegar to boil in saucepan, add ingredients.
3. Cook on medium heat for 10 minutes while stirring.
4. Reduce, simmer on low for 30 minutes.
5. Cool, pour into jars leaving 1/2" headspace.
6. Process and store for up to a year.

{preparation + cook time 30 mins makes 1 ½ pints}

Sweet Eggplant Chutney

Suggested Jar: Regular Mouth, Half Pint

1-½ lb eggplant
1-½ lb tomato
4 cloves garlic, peeled and sliced
1 red onion, peeled and sliced
1 tsp oregano
1 cup brown sugar
1 cup red wine vinegar
1 tsp sea salt
olive oil

1. Blanch tomatoes, peel and chop.
2. Heat olive oil, add onions, garlic and eggplant and sauté for five minutes.
3. Add remaining ingredients, bring to boil.
4. Reduce heat, simmer for one hour.
5. Pour into jars leaving ½" headspace and process.

{preparation + cook time 30 mins **makes** 1 ½ pints}

Gooseberry Chutney

Suggested Jar: Wide Mouth, Pint

1 lb gooseberries
1 red onion, peeled and chopped
2 cloves garlic, peeled and chopped
1 cup brown sugar
½ cup raisins
1 cup balsamic vinegar
1 tsp cracked black pepper

1. Wash and sterilize jars.
2. Bring vinegar to boil, add sugar and stir for two minutes.
3. Add remaining ingredients and bring back to a boil.
4. Turn heat to low and simmer for 30 minutes.
5. Pour into jars and refrigerate for up to two weeks.

{preparation + cook time 1 hour makes 1 pint}

Grape Sesame Chutney

Suggested Jar: Regular Mouth, Pint

3 lbs seedless grapes
2 sweet onions, diced
1/2 cup dates, pitted and chopped
1/2 cup sesame seeds
1 cup brown sugar
1 tbsp sea salt
2 cups red wine vinegar

1. Wash and sterilize bottles.
2. Bring vinegar to a boil, add remaining ingredients save the grapes and cook for 10 minutes.
3. Add grapes, bring to boil, reduce heat and simmer for 40 minutes.
4. Pour into jars leaving 1/2" headspace.
5. Pat down to ensure there are no air pockets.
6. Seal and process in water bath.
7. Cool and store for up to a year.

{preparation + cook time 1 hour makes 2 quarts}

Jalapeno Peach Chutney

Suggested Jar: Regular Mouth, Pint

3 lbs peaches
1/2 lb jalapeños, seeded and chopped
1 red bell pepper, seeded and chopped
1 sweet onion, peeled and chopped
1 cup brown sugar
1 tbsp sea salt
2 cups red wine vinegar
olive oil

1. Wash and sterilize jars.
2. Blanch peaches, remove skin, pit and slice.
3. Bring vinegar to a boil, add remaining ingredients save the peaches and cook for 10 minutes.
4. Add peaches, bring to boil, reduce heat and simmer for 20 minutes.
5. Scoop chutney into jars leaving ½" headspace, seal and process.
6. Store for at least one week before opening in order to develop flavours.

{preparation + cook time 1 hour makes 2 quarts}

Summer Melon Chutney

Suggested Jar: Regular Mouth, Pint

3 lbs melon, diced
1/2 cup mint
1 lemon, juiced
1 cup brown sugar
1 tbsp sea salt
2 cups red wine vinegar

1. Wash and sterilize bottles.
2. Bring vinegar to a boil, add remaining ingredients save the grapes and cook for 10 minutes.
3. Add grapes, bring to boil, reduce heat and simmer for 40 minutes.
4. Pour into jars leaving 1/2" headspace.
5. Pat down to ensure there are no air pockets.
6. Seal and process in water bath.
7. Cool and store for up to a year.

{preparation + cook time 1 hour makes 2 quarts}

Orange Cherry Chutney

Suggested Jar: Regular Mouth, Half Pint

2 cups cherries, stemmed and pitted
1 cup orange slices
1 onion, peeled and chopped
1/2 cup molasses
1 cup red wine vinegar
1 tsp sea salt
1/2 tbsp crushed black pepper
1 cinnamon stick

1. Wash and sterilize jar.
2. Place red wine vinegar in large skillet and bring to boil.
3. Add sugar and stir for five minutes.
4. Add remaining ingredients and bring to a boil.
5. Reduce heat to low and cook for 30 minutes.
6. Remove cinnamon stick
7. Pour into jars leaving 1/2" headspace.
8. Process and store for up to 6 months.

{preparation + cook time 1 hour makes 1 quart}

Orange Sesame Chutney

Suggested Jar: Regular Mouth, Half Pint

8 cups orange segments, chopped (fresh or frozen)
1/2 cup sesame seeds
1/2 tsp paprika
1 tsp salt
2 tbsp brown sugar
1 cup cider vinegar

1. Wash and sterilize jar.
2. Place ingredients in blender.
3. Mix until chutney has some liquid but is still slightly chunky.
4. Pour into jars, refrigerate and use within three days.

{preparation + cook time 20 mins makes 1 pint}

Passionfruit Chutney

Suggested Jar: Regular Mouth, Half Pint

8 cups passion fruit flesh
1/2 cup almonds, chopped
1/2 cup sugar
1 cup red wine vinegar
1 tsp salt

1. Wash and sterilize jar.
2. Place red wine vinegar in large skillet and bring to boil.
3. Add sugar and stir for five minutes.
4. Add remaining ingredients and bring to a boil.
5. Reduce heat to low and cook for 30 minutes.
6. Cool.
7. Pour into jars leaving 1/2" headspace.
8. Process and store for up to 6 months.

{**preparation + cook time** 1 hour **makes** 1 pint}

Pear Ginger Chutney

Suggested Jar: Regular Mouth, Pint

2 lbs pears, peeled and chopped
2 red onions, peeled and chopped
1 cup dates, pitted and chopped
½ cup cranberries
1 cup brown sugar
1/2 tbsp sea salt
2 cups cider vinegar
1/2 tsp cinnamon

1. Wash and sterilize jars and lids.
2. Sweat pears and onions in large skillet over medium heat.
3. Stir in remaining ingredients save vinegar.
4. Add vinegar and reduce for five minutes.
5. Turn heat to low and allow to simmer for 45 minutes.
6. Pour into jars leaving ¼" headspace, clean rims, apply band, lids and process.
7. Store for up to three months

{preparation + cook time 1.5 hours **makes** 3 pints}

Peanut Chutney

Suggested Jar: Regular Mouth, Half Pint

1.5 cup peanuts, crushed
2 red onion, peeled and diced
2 cups distilled vinegar
1 red chilli pepper
1 cup brown sugar
1 tsp sea salt

1. Bring vinegar to boil in saucepan, add ingredients.
2. Cook on medium heat for 10 minutes while stirring.
3. Reduce, simmer on low for 30 minutes.
4. Cool, pour into jars leaving 1/2" headspace.
5. Process and store for up to a year

{**preparation + cook time** 1.5 hours **makes** 1 ½ pints}

Pineapple Coconut Chutney

Suggested Jar: Wide Mouth, Pint

2 cups coconut, grated (fresh is best)
2 cups pineapple chunks
1 red onion, peeled and diced
½ cup brown sugar
½ cup vinegar
1 tbsp ginger, grated
1 tsp sea salt

1. Combine coconut, pineapple and red onion in blender, leave slightly chunky.
2. Bring vinegar to boil, mix in sugar, ginger and sea salt, cook for five minutes on medium.
3. Once vinegar mixture has cooled add to coconut blend and pulse for a minute.
4. Allow mixture to sit for 12 hours before refrigerating.
5. Use within two weeks.

{**preparation + cook time** 30 mins **makes** 2 pints}

Fiery Pineapple Chutney

Suggested Jar: Regular Mouth, Pint

2 lbs pineapple chunks
1/2 lb jalapeños, seeded and chopped
2 red onions, peeled and diced
1 cup brown sugar
1 tbsp sea salt
2 cups cider vinegar

1. Wash and sterilize jars.
2. Bring vinegar to a boil, add remaining ingredients save pineapple and cook for 10 minutes.
3. Add pineapple, bring to boil, reduce heat and simmer for 30 minutes.
4. Cool and scoop into jars leaving ½" headspace.
5. Process and store.

{preparation + cook time 1 hour makes 3 pints}

Pumpkin Spice Chutney

Suggested Jar: Regular Mouth, Half Pint

3 cups pumpkin, steamed
1.5 cups cider vinegar
1 onion, peeled and diced
1/2 cup dates, pitted and chopped
1/2 cup brown sugar
1 cinnamon stick
4 cloves

1. Bring vinegar to boil in saucepan, add remaining ingredients.
2. Cook on medium heat for 10 minutes while stirring.
3. Reduce, simmer on low for 30 minutes.
4. Remove cinnamon stick.
5. Cool, pour into jars leaving 1/2" headspace.
6. Process and store for up to a year.

{preparation + cook time 1 hour makes 1 ½ pints}

Raspberry Arugula Chutney

Suggested Jar: Regular Mouth, Pint

3 lbs raspberries
1 cup arugula, chopped
1 sweet onion, peeled and chopped
1/2 cup unsalted sunflower seeds
1 cup brown sugar
1/2 tbsp sea salt
2 cups cider vinegar

1. Wash and sterilize bottles.
2. Bring vinegar to a boil, add remaining ingredients save the grapes and cook for 10 minutes.
3. Add grapes, bring to boil, reduce heat and simmer for 40 minutes.
4. Pour into jars leaving 1/2" headspace.
5. Pat down to ensure there are no air pockets.
6. Seal and process in water bath.
7. Cool and store for up to a year

{preparation + cook time 1 hour makes 1 ½ quarts}

Green Tomato Chutney

Suggested Jar: Regular Mouth, Pint

3 lbs green tomatoes
2 onions, peeled and diced
4 cloves garlic, peeled and minced
1 red chilli pepper
1 cup brown sugar
1 tbsp sea salt
2 cups red wine vinegar

1. Wash and sterilize bottles.
2. Blanch green tomatoes and peel.
3. Bring vinegar to a boil, add remaining ingredients save the green tomatoes and cook for 10 minutes.
4. Add tomatoes, bring to boil, reduce heat and simmer for 40 minutes.
5. Pour into jars leaving 1/2" headspace.
6. Pat down to ensure there are no air pockets.
7. Seal and process in water bath.
8. Cool and store for up to a year.

{preparation + cook time 1 hour makes 2 quarts}

Tomato Basil Chutney

Suggested Jar: Regular Mouth, Pint

2 lbs tomatoes,
2 onions, peeled and chopped
2 cloves garlic, peeled and chopped
1/2 cup fresh basil, chopped
1 cup brown sugar
1 tbsp sea salt
1 tsp paprika
2 cups red wine vinegar

1. Wash and sterilize jars and lids.
2. Blanch tomatoes and peel.
3. Sweat tomatoes and onions in large skillet over medium heat.
4. Stir in remaining ingredients save vinegar.
5. Add vinegar and reduce for five minutes.
6. Turn heat to low and allow to simmer for 45 minutes.
7. Pour into jars leaving ¼" headspace, clean rims, apply band, lids and process.
8. Store for up to three months.

{**preparation + cook time** 1 hour **makes** 3 pints}

Farmhouse Preserves

A Preserve is a term used to describe all types of jams and jellies.
It is a thick cooked mixture which contains whole or cut up pieces of fruit and vegetables, commonly using pectin, sugar or honey as a gelling agent.
Just one spoonful can transform a drab dish into something sensational.

Autumn Spiced Apple Jam

Suggested Jar: Regular Mouth, Half Pint

4 cups apples, peeled and chopped
1 cup walnuts
1 tsp cinnamon
1 tsp cloves
1/2 cup honey
1/2 cup sugar
1/2 tsp sea salt
1/2 cup water

1. Wash and sterilize jars.
2. Place nuts in food processor and blend until mixture turns into chunky butter.
3. Place saucepan over medium-heat, add apples, water and cook for five minutes.
4. Add walnuts and cook for five minutes.
5. Add remaining ingredients and cook for another 10 minutes
6. Pack mixture into 1/2 pint jars and process.
7. Allow to cool for 12 hours before opening jar.

{**preparation + cook time** 30 mins **makes** 2 pints}

Green Apple Preserve

Suggested Jar: Regular Mouth, Pint

8 cups apples, peeled, cored, chopped
1 tsp ground cinnamon
3 cups sugar
2 oz dry pectin

1. Wash and sterilize bottles.
2. Heat saucepan to medium, add chopped apples.
3. Cook until apples soften.
4. Add sugar and ground cinnamon, cook for 10 minutes.
5. Add pectin and cook for 3 minutes.
6. Allow to cool, pour into jars and seal.

{**preparation + cook time** 30 mins **makes** 4 pints}

Aunty Alsa's Apricot Preserve

Suggested Jar: Regular Mouth, Pint

4lbs apricots, pitted and chopped
3 cups sugar
1 vanilla bean
2 pkg orange Jello

1. Wash canning jars thoroughly and sterilize in water bath or dishwasher.
2. Combine all items except for Jello in a pot and boil for 15 minutes.
3. Stir in Jello.
4. Pour mixture into jars, screw on band and lids.
5. Return jars to sterilization pot and boil for 15 minutes.
6. Remove from pot, store in cool space.
7. Preserve will be good for one year.

{preparation + cook time 1 hour makes 4 pints}

Cardamom Apricot Jam

Suggested Jar: Regular Mouth, Half Pint

8 cups apricots, seeded and quartered
1 tsp crushed cardamom
2 tbsp Whiskey
3 cups sugar
1 pkg dry pectin

1. Wash and sterilize bottles.
2. Combine all ingredients save pectic and allow to sit for 10 mins.
3. Place pot on medium-heat and add apricot mixture.
4. Cook until apricots are softened and begin to caramelize.
5. Add sugar and cook for 10 minutes.
6. Add pectin and cook for 3 minutes.
7. Allow to cool, pour into jars, seal and allow to rest for 48 hours before opening jars.

{**preparation + cook time** 1 hour **makes** 4 pints}

Honey Bee's Apricot Jam

Suggested Jar: Regular Mouth, Pint

2 lbs apricots
¼ cup honey
1 cup sugar
1 tsp sea salt
1 pkg dry pectin

1. Wash and sterilize jars.
2. Place all items save pectin in saucepan and cook down for 10 minutes.
3. Add pectin and cook for two minutes.
4. Pour into jars and process.
5. Place in cool space and wait five days before opening.

{**preparation + cook time** 30 mins **makes** 4 pints}

Basil Jelly

Suggested Jar: Wide Mouth, Half Pint

4 cups fresh basil, chopped
1 pkg Green Apple Jello
1-½ cup sugar

1. Wash and sterilize jars.
2. In a medium-saucepan, bring basil and sugar to a boil.
3. Add Jello, mix and remove from burner.
4. Spoon into jars and process.

{**preparation + cook time** 20 mins **makes** 2 pints}

Berry Medley Preserve

Suggested Jar: Regular Mouth, Pint

6 cups blueberries
4 cups fresh strawberries
3 cups sugar
2 pkgs strawberry Jello
1 vanilla bean

1. Thoroughly wash canning jars and sterilize in water bath or dishwasher.
2. Place fruit, sugar and vanilla bean in a large pot and bring to boil.
3. Continue to cook for 10 minutes.
4. Stir in jello mixes.
5. Fill jars with fruit mixture, close up with bands and lids.
6. Process jars in water bath.
7. Remove, allow to cool and store

{**preparation + cook time** 30 mins **makes** 4 pints}

Blueberry and Honey Jam

Suggested Jar: Wide Mouth, Pint

1 lb blueberries
1/2 cup honey
1 tsp vanilla beans
½ cup water
1 pkg pectin

1. Place blueberry in skillet and cook for two minutes over medium heat.
2. Add honey, vanilla beans and water, cook covered on low for 10 minutes.
3. Add pectin, cook for another two minutes.
4. Cool for 3 hours.
5. Spoon into jars, seal and process.

{preparation + cook time 30 mins makes 2 pints}

Cardamom Carrot Jam

Suggested Jar: Regular Mouth, Half Pint

8 cups carrots, shredded,
2 tsp crushed cardamom
3 cups sugar
½ cup water
1 pkg dry pectin

1. Wash and sterilize bottles.
2. Combine all ingredients save pectic and allow to sit for 10 mins.
3. Place pot on medium-heat and add carrot mixture.
4. Cook until carrots are softened and partially mash.
5. Add sugar and cook for 10 minutes.
6. Add pectin and cook for 3 minutes.
7. Allow to cool, pour into jars, seal and allow to rest for 24 hours before opening jars.

{**preparation + cook time** 30 mins **makes** 4 pints}

Carrot Apple Jam

Suggested Jar: Wide Mouth, Pint

4 cups apples, peeled and chopped
4 cups carrots, peeled and grated
1 tsp cinnamon
2 cups brown sugar
1 pkg dry pectin

1. Wash and sterilize bottles.
2. Heat saucepan to medium, add chopped apples and cook for two minutes.
3. Add carrots and cook for five minutes while continuously stirring.
4. Add cinnamon, sugar and bring to a boil,
5. Add pectin and cook for 3 minutes.
6. Allow to cool, pour into jars and seal.

{**preparation + cook time** 30 mins **makes** 4 pints}

Carrot and Pistachio Jam

Suggested Jar: Wide Mouth, Pint

1 lb carrots, grated
1 cup honey
2 tbsp pistachio, crushed
1 tsp cardamom, ground
½ cup water
1 pkg pectin

1. Place carrots in skillet and cook for two minutes over medium heat.
2. Add pistachio, cardamom and water, cook covered on low for 10 minutes.
3. Add pectin, cook for another two minutes.
4. Cool for 3 hours.
5. Spoon into jars, seal and process.

{preparation + cook time 30 mins makes 2 pints}

Festive Cherry Mint Preserve

Suggested Jar: Wide Mouth, Pint

8 cups cherries
1/4 cup mint, pureed
4 cups sugar
2 oz dry pectin

1. Wash and sterilize bottles.
2. Heat saucepan to medium, add chopped cherries and mint.
3. Cook until cherries soften, mash cherries.
4. Add sugar, cook for 10 minutes.
5. Add pectin and cook for 3 minutes.
6. Allow to cool, pour into jars and seal.

{**preparation + cook time** 30 mins **makes** 4 pints}

Coca Mint Jam

Suggested Jar: Regular Mouth, Half Pint

1 lb mint, washed and chopped
1 cup cocoa
1 vanilla bean
1/2 tsp sea salt
1/2 cup water
1 pk dry pectin

1. Wash and sterilize jars
2. Slit open vanilla bean and separate seeds from pod.
3. Puree mint.
4. Place saucepan over medium-heat, add mint, water and cook for five minutes.
5. Add remaining ingredients save pectin and cook for another 5 minutes.
6. Remove vanilla pod, add pectin and cook for 2 minutes.
7. Pack mixture into half pint jars and process.
8. Allow to cool for 12 hours before opening jars.

{preparation + cook time 30 mins **makes** 1 pint}

Fig and Walnut Jam

Suggested Jar: Wide Mouth, Pint

1 lb figs
1 cup brown sugar
2 tbsp walnuts, crushed
1 tsp cloves, ground
½ cup water
1 pkg pectin

1. Place figs in skillet and cook for two minutes over medium heat.
2. Add, walnuts, cloves and water, cook covered on low for 10 minutes.
3. Add pectin, cook for another two minutes.
4. Cool for 3 hours.
5. Spoon into jars, seal and process.

{**preparation + cook time** 30 mins **makes** 2 pints}

Garlic Preserve

Suggested Jar: Wide Mouth, Pint

4 head garlic
1 lemon, juiced
2 cups extra virgin olive oil

1. Preheat oven to 350 degrees.
2. Peel garlic and remove ends.
3. Spread garlic in roasting tray and cover with 1/2 cup olive oil.
4. Roast for 20 minutes.
5. Add remaining olive oil and lemon juice, mix and pour into jar.
6. Refrigerate.

{**preparation + cook time** 50 mins **makes** 1 pint}

Sweet'n Smokin' Jalapeno Jelly

Suggested Jar: Regular Mouth, Half Pint

4 green peppers, chopped
3 jalapeno peppers, seeded
2 cups vinegar
6 cups sugar
1 tsp sea salt
2 pkgs liquid pectin

1. Wash and sterilize jars
2. Place all items save vinegar and liquid pectin in food processor, blend.
3. Allow mixture to sit for 10 minutes.
4. Place pot over medium-heat and pour in jalapeno mixture.
5. Bring to boil, cook for 10 minutes.
6. Add vinegar and stir in pectin and bring back to boil.
7. Remove from stove, pour into jars, leave 1/2" headspace.
8. Seal in water canner and store.

{**preparation + cook time** 1 hour **makes** 4 pints}

Bourbon Sunrise Peach Jam

Suggested Jar: Regular Mouth, Half Pint

8 cups peaches, peeled and chopped
1 vanilla bean pod
1 tbsp Bourbon
3 cups sugar
1 pkg dry pectin

1. Wash and sterilize bottles.
2. Combine all ingredients save pectic and allow to sit for 10 mins.
3. Place pot on medium-heat and add peach mixture.
4. Cook until peaches are softened and begin to caramelize.
5. Slit open vanilla bean pod and add seeds into mixture.
6. Add sugar and cook for 10 minutes.
7. Add pectin and cook for 3 minutes.
8. Allow to cool, pour into jars and seal.

{preparation + cook time 1 hour **makes** 4 pints}

Peachy Pyjama Preserve

Suggested Jar: Regular Mouth, Half Pint

10 cups fresh peaches
3 cups sugar
2 pkgs Orange Jello
1 vanilla bean
1 cup walnuts, chopped

1. Thoroughly wash canning jars sterilize.
2. Place fruit, sugar and vanilla bean in a large pot and bring to boil.
3. Continue to cook for 10 minutes.
4. Stir in jello mixes and cook for two minutes, cool.
5. Fill jars with fruit mixture, seal and process.
6. Store for up to one year.

{preparation + cook time 30 mins makes 4 pints}

Honey Peach Preserve

Suggested Jar: Regular Mouth, Half Pint

8 cups peaches, peeled and chopped
1 tsp vanilla bean
3 cups sugar
2 oz dry pectin

1. Wash and sterilize bottles.
2. Heat saucepan to medium, add chopped peaches.
3. Cook until peaches are melted into a chunky sauce.
4. Slit open vanilla bean pod, and add seeds into mixture.
5. Add sugar and cook for 10 minutes.
6. Add pectin and cook for 3 minutes.
7. Allow to cool, pour into jars and seal.

{**preparation + cook time** 30 mins **makes** 4 pints}

Foot Stompin' Peach and Amaretto Jam

Suggested Jar: Wide Mouth, Half Pint

1-½ lb peaches
2 cups water
½ cup Amaretto
3 cups cane sugar

1. Blanch peaches, peel, remove stones and chop.
2. Cook peaches in skillet over medium heat for five minutes.
3. Add water, sugar and simmer covered on 10 minutes on low.
4. Turn off heat, mix in Amaretto and allow to cool.
5. Spoon into jars leaving ¼" headspace, seal, process and store

{**preparation + cook time** 30 mins **makes** 2 pints}

Pear and Bourbon Jam

Suggested Jar: Wide Mouth, Half Pint

1 lb pear, peeled, cored and diced
1 cup brown sugar
3 tbsp Bourbon
1 pkg pectin

1. Place pears in skillet and cook for two minutes over medium heat.
2. Add sugar, bourbon and water, cook covered on low for 10 minutes.
3. Add pectin, cook for another two minutes.
4. Cool for 3 hours.
5. Spoon into jars, seal and process.

{**preparation + cook time** 30 mins **makes** 2 pints}

Pear Walnut Jam

Suggested Jar: Regular Mouth, Half Pint

4 cups pears, peeled and chopped
1 cup walnuts
1 vanilla bean
1/2 cup honey
1/2 cup sugar
1/2 tsp sea salt
1/2 cup water

1. Wash and sterilize jars.
2. Place nuts in food processor and blend until mixture turns into chunky butter.
3. Slit open vanilla bean and remove seeds.
4. Place saucepan over medium-heat, add pears, water and vanilla shell and seeds and cook for five minutes.
5. Remove vanilla shell, add walnuts and cook for five minutes.
6. Add remaining ingredients and cook for another 10 minutes
7. Pack mixture into half pint jars and process.
8. Allow to cool for 12 hours before opening jar.

{**preparation + cook time** 1 hour **makes** 2 pints}

Plucky Plum Jam

Suggested Jar: Wide Mouth, Half Pint

4 lbs plums
1 Serrano chili
1 cup dates, pitted and chopped
1 cup brown sugar
1 cup white wine vinegar

1. Blanch plums and peel.
2. Bring vinegar to boil, add plums and cook on medium for 10 minutes.
3. Add remaining ingredients, bring up to boil.
4. Reduce heat to low, cover and allow to simmer for 30 minutes.
5. Remove serrano chilli, cool and scoop into jars leaving 1/2" headspace.
6. Process and store for up to a year.

{**preparation + cook time** 1 hour **makes** 3 ½ pints}

Walnut Pumpkin Preserve

Suggested Jar: Wide Mouth Half Pint

8 cups pumpkin, steamed, peeled and chopped
1 vanilla bean
4 cups sugar
2 oz dry pectin

1. Wash and sterilize bottles.
2. Heat saucepan to medium, add chopped pumpkin
3. And reduce to sauce.
4. Add sugar and vanilla bean, cook for 10 minutes.
5. Remove vanilla bean,
6. Add pectin and cook for 3 minutes.
7. Allow to cool, pour into jars and seal.

{preparation + cook time 30 mins makes 4 pints}

Red Bell Pepper Preserve

Suggested Jar: Regular Mouth, Half Pint

2 cups red bell pepper, julienned
4 cloves garlic, peeled
1 lemon, juiced
2 cups extra virgin olive oil

1. Preheat oven to 350 degrees.
2. Spread bell pepper in roasting tray and cover with 1/2 cup olive oil.
3. Roast for 20 minutes.
4. Add remaining olive oil and lemon juice, mix and pour into jar.
5. Refrigerate.

{**preparation + cook time** 1 hour **makes** 1 pint}

Raspberry Almond Jam

Suggested Jar: Regular Mouth, Half Pint

2 cups raspberries
1 cup water
4 cups sugar
1/2 cup basil, chopped
1 pkg dry pectin

1. Mash raspberries.
2. Heat saucepan, add raspberries and water, cook for 5 minutes.
3. Stir in basil and sugar, cook for 5 minutes.
4. Mix in pectin and cook for five minutes.
5. Cool, spoon into jars and process.

{**preparation + cook time** 30 mins **makes** 1 pint}

Ruth's Raspberry Coca Jam

Suggested Jar: Regular Mouth, Half Pint

4 lbs raspberries
3/4 cup cocoa
1 vanilla bean
1/2 tsp sea salt
1/2 cup water
1 pk dry pectin

1. Wash and sterilize jars
2. Slit open vanilla bean and separate seeds from pod.
3. Place saucepan over medium-heat, add raspberries, water and cook for five minutes.
4. Add remaining ingredients save pectin and cook for another 5 minutes.
5. Remove vanilla pod, add pectin and cook for 2 minutes.
6. Pack mixture into half pint jars and process.
7. Allow to cool for 12 hours before opening.

{preparation + cook time 30 mins makes 3 pints}

Strawberry Field's Coca Preserve

Suggested Jar: Regular Mouth, Half Pint

2 cups strawberries, hulled
1 cup water
4 cups sugar
1 tbsp cocoa powder
1 pkg dry pectin

1. Mash strawberries.
2. Heat saucepan, add strawberries and water, cook for 5 minutes.
3. Stir in cocoa and sugar, cook for 5 minutes.
4. Add 1 pkg pectin, stir for a minute.
5. Remove from heat, pour into jars.
6. Process and store.

{**preparation + cook time** 30 mins **makes** 1 pint}

Strawberry Vanilla Preserve

Suggested Jar: Regular Mouth, Half Pint
10 cups fresh strawberries
3 cups sugar
2 pkgs strawberry Jello
1 vanilla bean

1. Thoroughly wash canning jars and fill with water.
2. Place jars in canning pot, fill pot with water and bring to boil to sterilize jars.
3. Place fruit, sugar and vanilla bean in a large pot and bring to boil.
4. Continue to cook for 10 minutes.
5. Stir in jello mixes.
6. Remove jars and fill with fruit mixture leaving ¼" headspace.
7. Process in water bath and store for up to one year.

{**preparation + cook time** 50 mins **makes** 4 pints}

Summer Rhubarb Preserve

Suggested Jar: Regular Mouth, Half Pint

9 cups rhubarb, chopped
2 cups strawberries
3 cups sugar
2 pkg strawberry Jello

1. Wash canning jars thoroughly and fill with water.
2. Place jars in pot or canning pot, ensure jars do not touch bottom of pot.
3. Add water to pot and boil for 10 minutes.
4. Combine all items except for Jell-o in a pot and boil for 15 minutes.
5. Mix in Jello.
6. Pour mixture into jars, screw on band and lids.
7. Return jars to sterilization pot and boil for 15 minutes.
8. Remove from pot, store for up to one year.

{preparation + cook time 1 hour makes 4 pints}

Trish's Tomato Jam

Suggested Jar: Regular Mouth, Half Pint

8 lbs ripe tomatoes
7 cups sugar
3 lemons

1. Wash and sterilize jars.
2. Dunk tomatoes in a pot of boiling water for a minute.
3. Peel and chop tomatoes.
4. Place tomatoes in large pot and cook over medium heat for 10 minutes.
5. Add 3 cups sugar and cook down for 10 minutes.
6. Add remainder of sugar and continue to cook for 25 minutes, stirring constantly.
7. Pour into jars, process, shelve for at least one week before opening.

{**preparation + cook time** 1 hour **makes** 4 pints}

Clint's Quince Jam

Suggested Jar: Regular Mouth, Pint

3 lbs quince, peeled and cored
¼ cup ginger, peeled and grated
½ cup raisins
½ cup dates, seeded and chopped
2 cups red wine vinegar
2 cups brown sugar
1 tbsp sea salt

1. Wash and sterilize jars.
2. Combine all ingredients in stockpot and cook over medium-heat for 10 minutes while stirring.
3. Bring ingredients to a boil, then reduce heat to low and allow to simmer for 45 minutes.
4. Cool on countertop for 12 hours.
5. Pour into canning jars, leaving ½" headspace and process.

{preparation + cook time 1.5 hours makes 4 pints}

Watermelon Mint Jam

Suggested Jar: Regular Mouth, Pint

6 lbs watermelon flesh, sliced
1 cup fresh mint
3 cups sugar
1 tbsp sea salt
2 pkgs dry pectin

1. Wash and sterilize jars.
2. Place all items save pectin in saucepan and cook on medium heat for 10-15 minutes.
3. Add pectin and cook for two minutes.
4. Pour into jars and process.
5. Place in cool space and wait five days before dipping in.

{**preparation + cook time** 30 mins
makes 4 pints}

Conversion Chart

Volumes

US Fluid Oz	US	Imperial	Millitres	Dry Oz	Pounds	Grams	Kilos
	1/2 teaspoon	1/2 teaspoon	2.5				
1/6	1 teaspoon	1 teaspoon	5				
1/4	2 teaspoons	1 dessert spoon	10	1		30	
1/2	1 tablespoon	1 tablespoon	15	2		60	
1	2 tablespoons	2 tablespoons	30	3		90	
2	1/4 cup	4 tablespoons	60	3 1/2		105	
4	1/2 cup		125	4	1/4	125	
5		1/4 pint	150	5		150	
6	3/4 cup		175	6		180	1/4
8	1 cup		250	8	1/2	250	
9			275	9		280	
10	1 1/4 cups	1/2 pint	300	12	3/4	360	1/2
12	1 1/2 cups		375	16	1	500	
15		3/4 pint	450	18		560	
16	2 cups		500	20	1 1/4	610	
18	2 1/4 cups		550	24 1/2	1 1/2	720	
20	2 1/2 cups	1 pint	600				
24	3 cups		750				

Quick Volumes

Pinch is less than 1/8 Teaspoon
1 metric Teaspoon – 5ml
1 metric Dessertspoon – 10ml
1 metric Tablespoon – 15ml
1 metric cup – 250ml
1000ml - 1 litre – 1 ¼ pints

Oven Temperatures

C	F	Oven
90	220	Very Cool
110	225	Cool
120	250	Cool
140	275	Cool - Moderate
150	300	Warm - Moderate
160	325	Medium
180	350	Moderate
190	375	Moderate - Hot
200	400	Fairly Hot
215	425	Hot
230	450	Very Hot
250	475	Very Hot
260	500	Very Hot

Weight Volumes

1 pound of flour - 3 ½ cups
1 pound of sugar – 2 ¼ cups
1 stick of butter is ¼ pound or 110 grams

Index

A

Auntie's Pickled Artichokes 11
Artichoke Carrot Pickle 27
Aunty Alsa's Ginger Pickle 46
Apple and Fig Chutney 67
Alsa's Sweet Pickle Relish 73
Apple Ginger Chutney 81
Autumn Spiced Apple Jam 106
Aunty Alsa's Apricot Preserve 108

B

Bread and Butter Pickles 17
Barnyard Beetroot Pickles 29
Bert's Beet and Cauliflower Pickle 31
Brussel Sprout Pickle 32
Balsamic Tomato Chutney 71
Basil Pine Nut Chutney 80
Banana Chutney 82
Blueberry Chutney 84
Basil Jelly 111
Berry Medley Preserve 112
Blueberry and Honey Jam 113
Bourbon Sunrise Peach Jam 122

C

Curried Pickled Eggs 9
Classic Spiced Pears 23
Carolina's Pickled Cukes 28
Cabbage Patch Pickle 35
Carrot Raisin Pickle 38
Cauliflower Mustard Pickles 42
Corn Freezer Pickle 43
Cherry Tomato Pickle 57
Caramelized Onion and Balsamic Chutney 70
Corn Relish 75
Christmas Chutney 77
Caramelised Onion and Apple Chutney 78
Carrot Raisin Chutney 85
Cherry Chutney 86
Cardamom Apricot Jam 109
Cardamom Carrot Jam 114
Carrot Apple Jam 115
Carrot and Pistachio Jam 116
Coca Mint Jam 118
Clint's Quince Jam 137

D

Dads Spicy Pickled Onions 8
Dads Mustard Onion Relish 72

E

English Style Pickled Onions 7
Easy Peazy Freezer Pickle 41

F

Farmhouse Dill Pickles 10
Farmhouse Preserved Lemons 14
Fancy-Schmancy Artichoke Heart Pickle 26
Festive Bell Pepper Pickle 34
Fig Tomato & Caramelized Onion Relish 66
Fresh Coriander Chutney 87
Fiery Pineapple Chutney 100
Festive Cherry Mint Preserve 117
Fig and Walnut Jam 119
Foot Stompin' Peach and Amaretto Jam 125

G

Grans Sweet Mustard Pickles 16
Green Tomato Pickles 24
Green Bean Pickle 33
Garlic Eggplant Pickle 45
Grandma's Okra Pickle 49
Green Tomato Relish 74
Green Chilli Chutney 88
Gooseberry Chutney 90
Grape Sesame Chutney 91
Green Tomato Chutney 103
Green Apple Preserve 107
Garlic Preserve 120

J

Jalapeno Peach Chutney 92

L

Lawnies Pickled Eggs 20

M

Minty Blueberry Pickle 30
Mad Dawg's Mushroom Farm Pickle 48
Mango Chutney 76
Minty Beetroot Chutney 83

O

Old Fashioned Pickled Eggplant 21
Orange Cherry Chutney 94
Orange Sesame Chutney 95

P

Pickled Jalapenos 12
Pickled Garlic 18
Pickled Carrot Sticks 19
Pickled Nectarines 22
Pickled Cauliflower and Onions 25
Purple Egg Pickle 44

H

Hot Tomato Pickle 60
Harpers Tomato Relish 64
Harpers BBQ Mushroom Relish 65
Honey Bee's Apricot Jam 110
Honey Peach Preserve 124

Q

Quick'n Easy Veg out Pickle 39

R

Red Pickled Cabbage 13
Red Pickled Ginger 15
Red Cabbage and Bell Pepper Pickle 36
Roasted Red Pepper Pickle 52
Radish Peppercorn Pickle 54
Roasted Pepper and Chili Tomato Relish 68
Raspberry Arugula Chutney 102
Red Bell Pepper Preserve 130
Raspberry Almond Jam 131
Ruth's Raspberry Coca Jam 132

S

Sweet Carolina's Carrot Ginger Pickle 37
Spicy Jalapeno Pickle 47
Strawberry Onion Pickle 55
Summer Fair Vege Pickle 61
Summer Fair Hickory Bacon Chutney 79
Sweet Eggplant Chutney 89
Summer Melon Chutney 93
Sweet'n Smokin' Jalapeno Jelly 121
Strawberry Field's Coca Preserve 133
Strawberry Vanilla Preserve 134
Summer Rhubarb Preserve 135

Pickled Banana Peppers 53
Pickled Green Tomatoes 56
Passionfruit Chutney 96
Pear Ginger Chutney 97
Peanut Chutney 98
Pineapple Coconut Chutney 99
Pumpkin Spice Chutney 101
Peachy Pyjama Preserve 123
Pear and Bourbon Jam 126
Pear Walnut Jam 127
Plucky Plum Jam 128

T

The Busy Supermom Pickle 40
The put it on everything Onion Pickle 50
The peachy keen Banana Pepper Pickle 51
Texas Tomatillo Pickle 58
Tomato Toss Pickle 59
Tomato Apple & Fig Relish 69
Tomato Basil Chutney 104
Trish's Tomato Jam 136

W

Walnut Pumpkin Preserve 129
Watermelon Mint Jam 138

Z

Zucchini Ginger Pickle 62

Made in the USA
San Bernardino, CA
13 July 2014